OUTDOOR LIFE

WILDERNESS SURVIVAL GUIDE

⊢ **THE EDITORS of** *Outdoor Life* ⊣

weldon**owen**

CONTENTS

SKILLS & TOOLS

CONTENTS

LOST IN THE WOODS

CONTENTS

EXTREME CONDITIONS

INTO THE WILD—AND OUT AGAIN.

These days, it's all too easy to think that survival skills are a lost and useless art—as practical as knowing how to plow with an ox. The reality is that modern life puts the unprepared in precarious situations. And perversely, just when we really need to know how to signal with smoke or build a fire in the rain—when we wander too far in the woods, lose our way, break down, fall down , or go down the wrong trail—the skills necessary to dig our way out of the hole have all but eroded away. Those are the problems this book addresses. When you have to survive for an hour or a long cold night or longer, you can. Lucky is the man who can spark flame and sleep soundly on a fire bed, ready for the long hike home in the morning.

SKILLS TOOLS

WHAT DO YOU NEED TO SURVIVE?

Fire, water, shelter, and food. The essentials are available anywhere, if you've got your wits and a few essential tools. Thanks to floatplanes and helicopters, we're going farther and farther into the wilds. When we get there, we rely too heavily on things that go blank when the batteries die. It's what you carry in your head and on your back that will ensure you get back to civilization in one piece. Having a few good survival skills comes in just as handy when you need to whip up a hot trail lunch as when you need to warm your frozen fingers enough to weave a brush raft. So the next time some city slicker chuckles at the dryer lint you're saving for DIY fire starter, just remind yourself: You may never need this stuff—until you do.

Ever heard of the "Ten Essentials"? The original list of ten essential outdoor items was drawn up in the 1930s for mountain climbers and outdoor enthusiasts. A Seattle-based group called the Mountaineers designed the list for two reasons. First, it gave people a list of gear to acquire in case of emergency. Second, it provided a support system in the event that someone had to unexpectedly stay outdoors overnight (or longer). The classic ten essentials are a map, compass, sunglasses and sunscreen (counted as one item), extra clothing, flashlight, first-aid supplies, fire starter, matches, knife, and extra food. The group has since updated the list by focusing on systems rather than specific items.

The original list has some useful selections, but jumping forward 80 years, the updated list has two game changers: Hydration and emergency shelter are the two most critical elements of survival (barring any first-aid items needed for injuries). Water and shelter are glaringly absent in the original Ten Essentials, but, thankfully for a new generation of outdoor adventurers, the updated list provides a great framework.

THE UPDATED TEN ESSENTIAL SYSTEMS

1. Navigation (map and compass)

2. Sun protection (sunglasses and sunscreen)

3. Insulation (extra clothing and outerwear)

4. Illumination (headlamp or flashlight)

5. First-aid supplies

6. Fire (waterproof matches, lighter, and candles)

7. Repair kit and tools (duct tape, multitool, and other tools)

8. Nutrition (extra food)

9. Hydration (extra water)

10. Emergency shelter

LIGHTEN YOUR PACK

You can prepare for a survival situation before you ever set foot in the woods. Efficient packing means if you get lost you've got less to carry. And even if you don't, a lighter pack is a good thing!

2 TO 3 POUNDS Replace your leather wafflestompers with a pair of midcut boots with synthetic uppers.

½ POUND Ditch the flashlight for a lightweight headlamp. Some models offer both a long-burning LED for doing your camp chores and a high-intensity beam for nighttime navigation.

3 POUNDS Trade your tent for a tarp shelter. You can find some tarp shelters that weigh less than 2 pounds.

1 POUND Leave the hatchet at home. Carry a wire saw.

2 POUNDS Cook with an ingenious wood-burning portable stove instead of a gas burner and avoid having to carry fuel.

1 TO 2 POUNDS Pack only two sets of clothes: one for camp, the other for hunting or fishing.

1 POUND Remove packaging from commercial food items. Repack in reclosable plastic bags and lightweight water bottles.

3 UPGRADE YOUR SURVIVAL KIT

Every personal survival kit should contain the fundamentals—waterproof matches, whistle, compass, knife, water-purifying tablets, a small flashlight. Think you have all your bases covered? See if you have room for a few of these low-volume lifesavers.

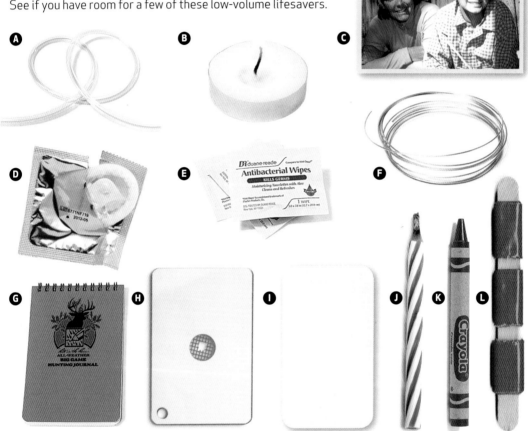

(A) SURGICAL TUBING Use it as a straw to suck water from shallow seeps, as a tourniquet, or as a means to blow a spark to flame. **(B) TEA LIGHT CANDLE** The longer-burning flame will light wet wood. **(C) SMALL PHOTO OF LOVED ONES** Thinking of family and friends helps keep survival instincts strong. **(D) UNLUBRICATED CONDOM** The best emergency canteen there is. **(E) ANTIBACTERIAL WIPES** Stave off infection with a single-use packet. **(F) WIRE** If you can't think of 10 ways to use this, you're not an outdoorsman to begin with. **(G) WATERPROOF PAPER** Leave a note for rescuers—even in a howling blizzard. **(H) SIGNAL MIRROR** On a clear day, a strong flash can be seen from 10 miles away. **(I) FRESNEL LENS** The size of a credit card, this clear lens will start a fire using sunlight. **(J) TRICK BIRTHDAY CANDLES** The wind can't blow them out. **(K) RED CRAYON** Mark trees as you move. You can also use the crayon as a fire starter. **(L) BLAZE ORANGE DUCT TAPE WOUND AROUND A TONGUE DEPRESSOR** Tear off 1-inch strips of tape to use as fire starters or route markers. Shave wood off the tongue depressor with your knife to use as tinder.

4 MAKE A KIT IN A CAN

You can pack a surprising amount of crucial gear in a very small container—even one as small as a mint tin—to create a highly portable BOB that fits in your backpack. Check military surplus stores for ideal containers (grenade canisters work nicely) and stock the following items:

- ☐ Small pen and paper
- ☐ First-aid instruction cards
- ☐ Duct tape
- ☐ Razor blades
- ☐ Wire saw
- ☐ Waterproof matches or fire starter
- ☐ Needle and thread

- ☐ Safety pins
- ☐ Water-purification tablets
- ☐ Zip ties
- ☐ Adhesive bandages
- ☐ Disinfectant wipes
- ☐ Micro compass
- ☐ Fishing kit (ten hooks, four split shot, two swivels, 25 feet [7.6 m] of 20-pound [9-kg] test line)
- ☐ Folded one-page guide to edible plants in your area
- ☐ 5 square feet (0.5 sq m) of aluminum foil
- ☐ Signal mirror
- ☐ Bouillon cubes
- ☐ Shoelaces
- ☐ Copper wire
- ☐ AA batteries
- ☐ Alcohol swabs
- ☐ Painkillers

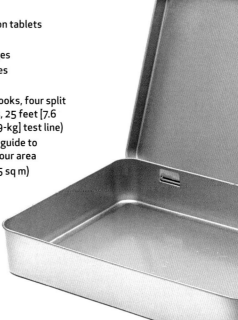

5 CARRY A COMPASS

The ancients found their way across entire seas with crude magnetic compasses, so there's no reason you can't find your way across a snowfield with basically the same tool. The modern compass allows travelers to move in a straight line even when a dark night or sudden snow squall removes all landmarks. Carry a compass and check it often, but be aware that a sensitive modern compass can react to nearby steel and other ferrous metal objects, such as gun barrels and even large belt buckles. Hold the compass away from magnetic metal objects for a true and honest reading.

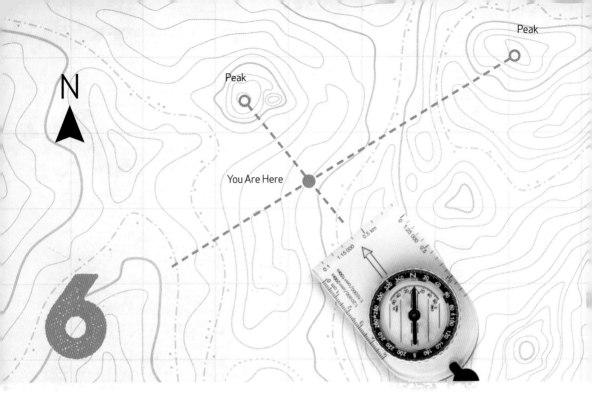

FIND YOURSELF ON A MAP

First things first: To use a map and compass successfully, you have to figure out just where you are on that map. Or to put it in outdoor geek terms, you need to triangulate a "fix" on your position.

KNOW WHICH WAY'S UP Paper maps are printed with north at the top. Using the compass, orient the map so it aligns with magnetic north.

FIND KEY LANDMARKS Once you have the map oriented, look around you for terrain features like a lake, river, or mountain peak. Identify the same features on the map.

PLOT A COURSE Looking up with your compass in hand, point the red arrow of the compass base plate (this is called "shooting a bearing" in orienteering speak) at the visible terrain feature. If the compass shows a bearing of, say, 320 degrees, draw a line from that feature on the map at an angle of 140 degrees (320 minus 180). You are somewhere on that line, called a line of position (LOP).

LAY A FOUNDATION You don't know where you are on that line until you shoot another bearing, preferably at something between 60 and 120 degrees from the first one. When you draw the second LOP on the map, extend it so it crosses the first one. Where the two LOPs intersect is your "fix." That's where you are. Once you know your position, other decisions, such as which way to walk, become much easier.

7 GET LOST-PROOF

We've all been a little lost at some point, whether we were willing to admit it or not, but here's the good part—getting lost is usually one of the easiest wilderness problems to prevent. So how do we lost-proof ourselves? See below. And always, always, make sure a responsible person knows where you are going and exactly when you are coming back—just in case you get stuck somewhere.

- Get a map of the area that you are traveling to and study it before going.

- Use the map and a compass (or GPS) while you are there and always stay aware of your position on the map.

- Imagine what the terrain would look like from a bird's-eye view and visualize your place in that terrain. Think of that little "You Are Here" arrow on the big map at a trailhead and keep it updated in your mind.

- Look behind you frequently, especially if you will be returning in that direction.

- Look for big, unusual landmarks and keep the them in view if possible.

- Study and remember the landmarks that you use.

- When traveling off the trails, use prominent, distant landmarks and/or a compass to travel in straight lines.

- Use a "handrail." This can be a river, ridge, or any other terrain feature that gives you guidance.

8 TAKE A BACK BEARING

The reading from a back bearing gives you a compass direction to follow to return to your starting position. More important, it can correct lateral drift off your intended direction of travel, which is what occurs each time an obstacle forces you to move off your intended line. Once you have your forward bearing, turn around 180 degrees and take a back bearing. (Say you're moving in a direction of travel of 45 degrees, or northeast. Your back bearing would be 225 degrees.)

As you move toward your destination, occasionally turn around and point the direction of travel arrow on your compass back to your last location. The white end of the compass needle should point there. If not, regain the correct line by moving until the needle lines up.

9 KNOW KNIVES TO SURVIVE

No other tool is called upon to perform as many tasks, in as many ways, under as many conditions, as the knife. It can take a life and save one. Cut cord, open the belly of an elk, help spark a fire, and skin a fish. A good knife is a tool, an icon, a symbol of its bearer's take on what it takes to live well—and sometimes simply survive—in the woods.

FIXED-BLADE KNIVES These knives are inherently strong due to the tang, the extension of the blade that carries into the knife handle. Also called sheath knives, fixed blades are easy to clean and quick to put into action. They have no moving parts to break or gunk up with hair, blood, or grit. And the sleek lines of a fixed blade knife speak to the essence of outdoors competence—simple elegance and deadly efficiency.

FOLDING-BLADE KNIVES Consider an option that can be smaller and easier to carry than fixed blade models. Larger folding blades with pocket clips and strong locking mechanisms are hugely popular. Many are designed to be opened with one hand through the use of a thumb stud or blade hole, and some are built with assisted-opening devices that propel the blade into a fixed position after the user opens it partway.

SPINE The back of the blade, most often unsharpened and unground. A thick spine gives a knife strength.

JIMPING Corrugated grooves in the blade spine, choil, or handle for increased grip and a no-slip feel.

THUMB RAMP An elevated hump on the spine of the blade near the handle. It provides increased control of the knife and reduced forearm fatigue during periods of extended use.

CHOIL The unsharpened edge of the blade between the end of the handle and the beginning of the edge bevel. Many knives have a finger indent at the choil to aid in choking up on the blade.

BELLY The curved arc as the sharpened edge nears the blade tip. A knife with a lot of belly will have a sagging, swooping profile, perfect for the sweeping cuts needed to skin big game.

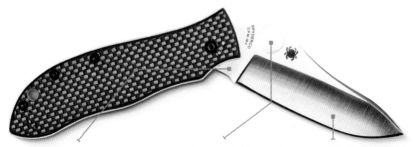

RICASSO The shank of the blade between the handle and the beginning of the sharpened edge. The ricasso often carries the maker's identifying mark, or "tang stamp."

THUMB HOLE OR STUD A hole in the spine or a stud that protrudes from the blade of a folding knife near the handle and allows the user to open the knife one-handed.

GRIND The finished shape of the blade when viewed in cross section. Hollow-grind blades have a concave shape and are easily sharpened, but tend to hang up in deep cuts. Flat-grind blades taper evenly from the spine to the cutting edge and hold an edge well.

THE SHAPE OF THINGS THAT CUT The shape of a blade determines how well that blade will perform specific tasks.

FILLET A thin, flexible blade allows the fillet knife to be worked over and around bones and fins.

CLIP POINT The classic general-use blade in which the spine of the blade drops in a concave curve to the tip (the "clip") to make a strong piercing point with a slightly upswept belly.

DROP POINT A downward convex curve along the blade spine forms a lowered point, which keeps the tip from cutting into an animal's organs during field dressing.

SKINNER The full curving knife belly is perfect for long, sweeping motions, such as skinning big game.

CAPER A short, pointed blade with a slightly downturned tip is easy to control in tight spots, such as removing the cape from an animal's head.

RECURVE The slight S-shaped belly forces the material being cut into the sharp edge. Recurves can be designed into most blade profiles.

10

THROW A KNIFE

Throwing a knife isn't difficult once you learn how to gauge the speed of rotation. Special throwing knives are unsharpened and have metal handles, but with practice—and caution—you can throw a hunting knife. Three tips: Keep your wrist stiff, use the same speed and motion for each throw, and step toward or away from the target until you find the distance where the rotation turns the knife point-first. Experts can accurately gauge up to seven rotations, but start with one and a half. This will result in a point-first direction with about a 4-yard (3.6-m) throw.

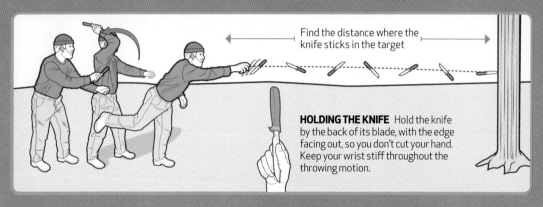

Find the distance where the knife sticks in the target

HOLDING THE KNIFE Hold the knife by the back of its blade, with the edge facing out, so you don't cut your hand. Keep your wrist stiff throughout the throwing motion.

11

CARE FOR YOUR KNIVES

Fixed-blade knives need only a quick wipe down with a damp cloth after each use and a light application of honing oil on the blade.

Folders and multitools collect blood and dirt at pivot points and locking mechanisms. If the tool has a plastic handle, immerse it in boiling water for 1 minute and then put it in a pot of warm water (so quick cooling doesn't crack the handle). Scrub nooks and crannies with a toothbrush, working pivot points back and forth, and then air-dry the knife before oiling. Use compressed air to blast out gunk.

Wipe away surface rust with an oily cloth or 0000 steel wool. Carbon blades naturally discolor with use. Bring them back to near-original luster by rubbing them with a cork dipped in cold wood ashes.

REMEMBER THE FOUR KNIFE "NEVERS"

NEVER store a knife in a leather sheath. It can cause rusting or discoloration.

NEVER use water to clean a horn handle. Horn absorbs moisture and can splinter.

NEVER use hot water to clean a wood handle. Rub it with olive oil.

NEVER touch the blade or metal parts after oiling. This can leave behind salt and acids, which can cause oxidation.

12 SURVIVE A ROUGH NIGHT USING A KNIFE

You can use a strong knife to turn a single conifer tree into an overnight bivvy. First, fell a 9-foot (2.75-m) balsam or other evergreen and remove all of the branches close to the trunk.

MAKE A BOUGH BED Cut the tips of the evergreen branches to 1 foot in length. Use wooden stakes to chock a 3-foot-long, 4-inch-diameter log (1-m, 10-cm), (cut from the tree trunk) where you want the head of your bed to be. Shingle the boughs at a 45-degree angle pointing away from the foot of the bed. Compress tightly as you work your way down. Anchor with a second 3-foot-long log from the trunk chocked with wooden stakes.

GLEAN TINDER The low, dead branches and sucker twigs of conifers make excellent tinder. Carve a fuzz stick from the thickest branch. Gather wood shavings from the others by scraping with the knife held at a 90-degree angle to the twigs.

GIN POLE A FISH To cook a fish when you have no utensils, snip away all twigs from the longest branch. Sharpen the fat end and drive it into the ground at about a 45-degree angle. Chock it with a rock or Y-shaped stick. Run cord through a fish's mouth and gill like a stringer, tie it to the branch, and let it dangle and cook beside the fire.

13

FELL A TREE WITH A KNIFE

A knife isn't as good as an axe in the backcountry. But when you're lost in the woods and it's your only friend, you can do a lot with a sturdy sheath knife—including felling a tree for a wickiup frame or firewood.

STEP 1 FROE AND MALLET Using a stout fixed-blade knife, hold the blade horizontally against the tree, with the cutting edge pointing slightly downward.

With a heavy stick, pound the blade into the trunk. Remove the blade from the trunk and make another cut with the blade turned slightly upward to remove a wedge of wood.

STEP 2 ROUND AND ROUND Completely girdle the tree this way. Don't bend it over until the cuts go all the way around or you'll splinter the wood, which makes it harder to cut.

STEP 3 PUSH AND SHOVE Once you've cut all the way around, give the trunk a shove. If it doesn't budge, remove more wedges.

14

SHARPEN A HATCHET OR AXE IN THE FIELD

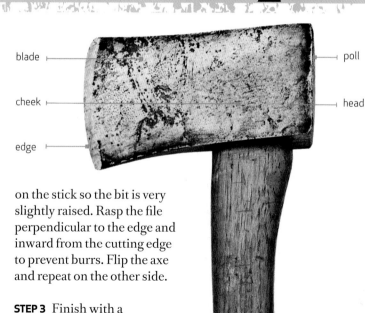

blade · ⊢ · poll

cheek · ⊢ · head

edge · ⊢

Assuming you have a file and whetstone in the toolbox, here's how to give your axe an edge.

STEP 1 Drive a peg into the ground. Place a wrist-thick stick 4 inches from the peg.

STEP 2 Place the poll of the axe against the peg, resting the cheek of the axe head on the stick so the bit is very slightly raised. Rasp the file perpendicular to the edge and inward from the cutting edge to prevent burrs. Flip the axe and repeat on the other side.

STEP 3 Finish with a whetstone. Use a circular motion that pushes the stone into the blade. Flip the axe and repeat.

15 MAKE WATERPROOF MATCHES

To make your own waterproof matches, use clear nail polish instead of paraffin wax. Nail polish is more durable and won't gunk up the match striker.

STEP 1 Fill a soft-drink bottle cap with nail polish (a).

STEP 2 Dip each match head into the polish (b) and then lay the match on the tabletop with its head extending off the edge (c).

STEP 3 Once the polish has dried, hold each match by the head and dip the entire remaining wooden portion of the match into the nail polish bottle (d).

STEP 4 Place matches on waxed paper to dry.

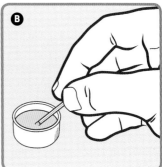
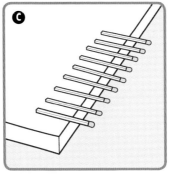

16

MAKE FIRE FROM ROCKS

To make a "fire stone" set, you'll need pieces of iron ore, such as bog iron or marcasite, and extremely fine tinder charred to improve ignition. True tinder fungus *(Fomes fomentarius)* is ideal if you can find it.

You'll need to scrape the tinder fungus with a sharp tool and place the fuzzy scrapings into a bundle of dry tinder.

Once you've done this, strike one piece of iron ore against the other briskly and quickly. You could also use a sharp piece of flint against the ore. Strike your sparks right over your tinder. If everything is just right, one of the tiny iron sparks will catch in the tinder, which can then be blown into a fire.

17 TIE A BUTTERFLY LOOP TO HANG GEAR

STEP 1 Hang a rope from your hand and coil it twice to form three coils (a). Move the right coil to the left, over the middle coil (b). The center coil now becomes the right coil.

STEP 2 Move this coil to the left over the top of the other two coils (c).

STEP 3 Take the coil you just moved to the left and pass it back to the right, under the remaining coils, to form a loop (d).

STEP 4 Pinch this loop against your palm, using your thumb to hold it. Slide your hand to the right, pulling this loop (e). Tighten by pulling both ends (f).

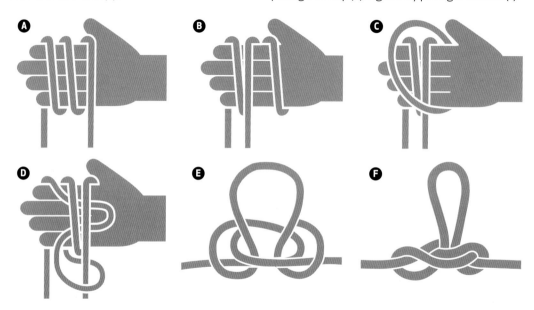

18 CARRY 50 FEET OF ROPE ON YOUR FEET

Real parachute cord is rated to 550 pounds. It's made of a tough outer sheath rated to 200 pounds, which protects seven interior strands, each rated to 50 pounds. Take apart a single 3-foot (1-m) length of paracord, and you'll have almost 25 feet (7.6 m) of cordage.

Use it to rig shelters and snares, lash knife blades to spears, fix broken tent poles—you name it. If you replace both laces with paracord when you buy a new pair of boots, you'll never be without a stash. Make sure you buy the 550-pound (250-kg)-test cord.

19 CUT PARACHUTE CORD WITH FRICTION

No knife? No problem. Tie the piece of parachute cord to be cut to two stout points—trees, truck bumpers, whatever. Leave plenty of slack. Take another few feet of cord (or the end of the line you're cutting if it's long enough) and place the middle of it over the piece of parachute cord to be cut. Grasp each end of this second piece firmly and saw back and forth. Friction will melt the parachute cord right where you want it cut.

20 TIE A BOWLINE KNOT

Forced to limit themselves to a single knot, most experts would choose the bowline (pronounced BOH-luhn), which is often called the King of Knots. It's jamproof—meaning it unties easily no matter what to—and it is very secure. It also can be tied one-handed, making it the knot of choice should you find yourself adrift in the water with an unconscious buddy to rescue. A running bowline (a bowline in which you simply pull the standing end of the line back through the finished knot) creates a noose suitable for snaring game. Still, the real reason to learn it is that to seamen, fire and rescue personnel, and others who live and die by the rope, all humanity can be divided into those who know how to tie a bowline and those who don't. And it's always better to be on the side that's in the know.

STEP 1 Remember the phrase: "The rabbit comes out of the hole, runs around the tree, and goes back in the hole." Make an overhead loop in your rope (the rabbit hole) and pull the working end (the rabbit) through the loop from the underside.

STEP 2 Circle that working end behind the rope above the loop (the tree) and then back through it.

STEP 3 Pull to tighten.

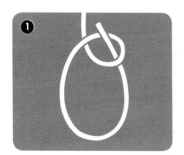
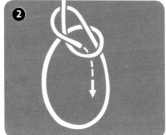
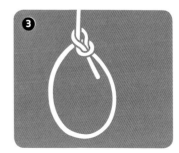

21 PREDICT THE WEATHER WITH PLANTS

Plants can tip you off that rain is on the way, usually because parts of them close as the moisture content in the air increases. (They don't want rain washing away their precious pollen reserves.) The plants here show their typical appearances on dry days (on the left) and rainy ones (on the right); look for these cues to avoid getting drenched.

SHAMROCK This three-leaved plant is comprised of sprigs of young clover. There is no true shamrock plant, but several varieties of clover are identified as such.

CHICORY Also called blue daisy, cornflower, and wild bachelor's buttons—this herbaceous perennial plant is a member of the dandelion family.

MORNING GLORY A species of bindweed, this vining plant twines around and climbs up other plants. In addition to blue, it also blooms in pink and white.

TEST YOUR LOCAL STONE

Razor-edged rocks are as close as your local creek, if you're in the right area and know how to break them. Not all rocks produce a good cutting edge when they break, and many have interiors that won't work for your purposes, so test them by delivering a quick tap with a hammer stone to break off a piece. This will show you the rock's interior and how it breaks, which is everything you need to know.

And you don't need to be a geologist to sort it all out: Flint, chert, jaspcr, chalcedony, quartz, and obsidian can all break to make sharp cutting tools. Just try out different types of local rock to see what works.

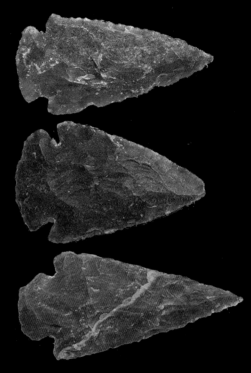

23

ROCK OUT WITH PERCUSSION

If you need some sharp, expedient blades (like for butchering), the easiest way to get them is using a method called bipolar percussion. In this method, you rest the stone you are trying to break on a large stone and strike it hard with a hammer rock. It's like being a blacksmith—the big rock is your anvil, providing unyielding resistance behind the breaking rock.

Stand your breaking rock on its tallest axis—this will allow the shock waves from the hammer stone to move through the rock via its most efficient path. For your hammer, use a large flat stone that's four to five times larger than the rock you are trying to break. If you're lucky, you'll fracture off some thin, wickedly sharp stone blades within a few strikes.

For any kind of stone tool work, make sure you wear gloves (preferably leather) and glasses or goggles to protect your hands and face—especially your eyes—from flying stone chips.

24 START A FIRE

BURNING SENSATIONS Always have a couple of these DIY options on hand.

INNER TUBE Three-inch strips or squares of bicycle inner tube burn with a rank, smoky flame hot enough to dry small kindling. No bike? Try the rubber squares in a wader-patch kit (don't forget the flammable patch glue) or a slice from a boot insole.

EGG CARTON AND SAWDUST Stuff each opening in a cardboard egg carton about half full of sawdust (collect this from your local school wood shop) and then add melted paraffin wax. Mix, let cool, and break apart.

DUCT TAPE A fist-size ball of loosely wadded duct tape is easy to light and will burn long enough to dry out tinder and kindling.

DRYER LINT Collect enough dryer lint to fill a gallon-size resealable bag halfway. Add ⅛ cup of citronella lamp fuel and squish it around to mix thoroughly.

EMERGENCY FLARE Cut a 2- to 4-inch section from an emergency road flare and seal the end with wax. It's easily lit even with wet gloves on.

COTTON BALLS AND PETROLEUM JELLY It's a Boy Scout standby because it works. Stuff petroleum jelly-soaked cotton balls into a film canister or waterproof pill bottle and you have several minutes of open flame at the ready.

NATURAL WONDERS Learn to identify and gather natural tinder in your neck of the woods.

SPANISH MOSS Not a moist moss at all, but an epiphytic, or "air plant," Spanish moss is a fast-catching tinder. But don't carry it around; it's notorious for harboring chiggers.

CEDAR BARK Common cedar bark should be worked over with a rock to smash the fibers. Pull the strands apart with your fingers and roll the material back and forth between your hands.

BIRCH BARK The flammable oils in the papery bark of birches make this a time-tested fire catcher. Strip ribbons of bark from downed trees; it works just as well as bark from live ones.

SAGEBRUSH BARK Pound strips of bark with a rock and then shred them between your palms and fashion a tinder basket.

CATTAIL FLUFF The cottony interior of a cattail spike can be fluffed into a spark-catching blaze. Have more tinder nearby because cattail fluff burns out quickly.

TINDER FUNGUS In northern areas, look for bulbous blotches of blackish wood on live birch trees. The inside of the fungus, which is reddish brown, easily catches a spark. Crumble it for a quick start to a fire or use chunks of it to keep a coal alive.

PUNK WOOD Rotten, dry wood will flame up with just a few sparks. Use a knife blade held at 90 degrees to file off punk dust and have larger pieces handy to transfer the sparks to larger punk wood that will burn with a coal.

25 MAKE CHAR CLOTH

Char cloth uses a process called pyrolysis (burning without oxygen) to turn cloth into a fire starter to use with flint and steel. It only takes a single spark. Here's how to make it.

STEP 1 Make a small hole in the top of a tin that closes tightly.

STEP 2 Fill the tin with scraps of cotton cloth (it needs to be all-natural; no synthetic fibers).

STEP 3 Place your container in the coals of a fire. Smoke should start streaming steadily out of the vent hole.

STEP 4 After 5 minutes of smoking, pull the tin off the coals. Let it cool before opening. The resulting cloth should be solid black and have a silky texture, but it should not fall apart. Now you have compact and lightweight tinder that you can carry with you until you need it for firestarting.

STEP 5 When you need tinder, pull the char cloth out and strike a single spark onto it. It should burn slowly and steadily.

STEP 6 Use the cloth to ignite your larger bundle of tinder.

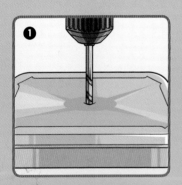

26 MAKE A FIRE KIT

Fire building is one of those skills that can make or break you in a survival situation. With so much riding on your ability to produce flame, it makes sense to plan for your own success by building a dedicated fire-starting kit. It's easy and fun to do, and you probably already have all the stuff lying around the house.

The three basic parts of this kit are the container, the heat/ignition sources, and the fuels. Note that the last two are plural—you're going to want some extra insurance in the form of multiple fire-starting implements and several fuels.

CONTAINER The container can be anything that's watertight and easily transported. This can range from a small Pelican case or similar waterproof box to a small wide-mouth plastic bottle or even a zip-top freezer bag.

IGNITION At a minimum, your kit should include a lighter, a box of matches, and a spark rod. The lighter is the best of the bunch for most fire-building situations. The open flame can be used to dry out damp tinder and kindling, catching it ablaze without much trouble. There really isn't a

situation in which matches are a better ignition source than a lighter, but I like the matchbox for redundancy and for the fact that those matchsticks can double as kindling. Last, the spark rod will serve as an indestructible backup ignition source. It won't light the variety of materials that matches and lighters will, but it will work when the lighter and matches have failed.

FUEL Dry cotton balls, dryer lint, or gauze can take the role of tinder (your initial fuel for the fire). You can also use a candle nub and a tube of petroleum jelly.

The candle can be lit and used as a fire starter by itself, or the wax can be dripped onto the tinder or kindling for a wet-weather fire boost. The petroleum jelly can be smeared into the cotton balls to make long-burning fire starters, plus the jelly is helpful for a number of first-aid and survival chores.

You could pre-assemble the petroleum jelly cotton balls, but the summertime heat can cause the jelly to melt and seep through all but the most watertight containers. Melted jelly ruins matchboxes. Carry the tightly sealed tube and the cotton balls separately.

27 MAKE A FIRE PLOUGH

This produces its own tinder by pushing out particles of wood ahead of the friction. Cut a groove in the softwood fireboard, then plough or rub the tip of a slightly harder shaft up and down the groove. The friction will push out dusty particles of the fireboard, which will ignite as the temperature increases.

Tinder ignites as temperature rises.

28

LEARN FIRE-MAKING BASICS

Where there's smoke there's fire? Not always, as someone nursing a poorly constructed fire finds out quickly. But if you want a steady blaze to cook on, keep animals away, or just warm up, follow these tips:

STEP 1 Prepare a spot with protection from wind and precipitation on dry ground (or a dry platform built up on moist ground).

STEP 2 You need three types of dry fuel: tinder, kindling, and larger pieces of wood. When you think of tinder, imagine a bird's nest, and bundle dry grasses into a nest shape. Kindling can range from the diameter of a matchstick up to the size of a wood pencil, so use splintered wood or small dry twigs snapped off a tree or shave pencil-size twigs into "fuzz sticks." For the larger pieces of wood, look for dry branches somewhere between the size of your finger and the size of your forearm. Shattered or split wood is best.

STEP 3 In a fire pit, build a tepee of kindling and place the tinder bundle beneath it. Don't construct it too tightly: the fire needs space to breathe. Have the larger pieces of wood close so they're handy when the fire is ready.

STEP 4 Kneel by the tinder and kindling, using your body as a windbreak. Light the tinder bundle and feed kindling into the fire until you have a strong blaze. When the fire is going strong, start adding the smallest wood, letting it catch fire and then gradually working up to the larger pieces.

29 MAKE A BOW DRILL

Of all the friction fire-starting methods, the bow drill is the most efficient at maintaining the speed and pressure needed to produce a coal and is the easiest to master. The combination of the right fireboard and spindle is the key to success in firestarting, so experiment with different types of dry softwoods until you find a set that produces. Remember that the drill must be as hard as or slightly harder than the fireboard.

STEP 1 Cut a notch at the edge of a round impression bored into the fireboard, as you would for a hand drill. Loosely affix the string to a stick bow, which can be any stout wood.

STEP 2 Place the end of a wood drill about the diameter of your thumb into the round impression. Bear down on the drill with a socket (a wood block or stone with a hollow ground into it), catch the drill in a loop of the bowstring, and then vigorously saw back and forth until the friction of the spinning drill produces a coal.

STEP 3 Drop the glowing coal into a bird's nest of very fine tinder, carefully lift the nest in your cupped hands, and give it a burst of oxygen by lightly blowing on it until it catches reliably on fire.

30 LEARN THE TRICKS TO TINDER

You can become a fire-building genius with a little know-how and some practice.

Use only dead stuff, nothing green, and have extra on standby. The center of your fire lay should be loaded with tinder, and it's this you light—not the wood. Make sure to block the wind with your body when lighting.

Pine, firs, spruce, and most other needle-bearing trees have sap in their wood. This is pitch, which is usually very flammable. Select dead twigs from these trees to get your fire going quickly even in damp weather. And pine needles make a good addition to tinder at any time because they light easily even when wet. Another tip? Douse your tinder with bug spray before lighting— it will add some serious flammability. Stand back.

31

START A FIRE WITH BINOCULARS

It's not easy, but it's not impossible, and if you're running out of options there's no harm in giving this a shot.

STEP 1 Disassemble the binoculars and remove one convex objective lens. Gather tinder, a stick to hold the tinder, some kindling, and a Y-shaped twig to hold the lens in place.

STEP 2 Arrange the tinder on the end of the small stick and put this on the ground. Having the tinder slightly elevated will increase airflow and flammability, and having it on the stick will allow you to move it to the area where the sun's rays are most concentrated.

STEP 3 Drive the Y-shaped stick into the ground and settle the lens inside its fork—carving some grooves will help. Focus the smallest point of intensified sunlight onto the tinder. It is critical that this focused beam not wobble. Once the tinder smolders, blow gently and have larger twigs ready to light.

32

MAKE A TINDER BUNDLE

Fire making does not end with the birth of a red-hot coal, nor does a glowing char cloth ensure that you're going to get a flame. You must transfer the coal or char cloth to a bundle of fine tinder before blowing it into flame. Good sources include dried grasses; lichens (including old man's beard); shavings from the inner bark of aspen, poplar, and cottonwood trees (which burn even when wet); and windblown seed or fluff. The tinder bundle should be roughly the size of a softball and loosely formed to allow air circulation.

To blow the bundle into a flame, make a small pocket in the center. Tuck the glowing coal or char cloth into the pocket and then loosely fold the edges around it. Next, pick up the bundle and gently blow on it. Once it has burst into flame, place it under a tepee formation of small twigs and add larger pieces until you establish a strong fire.

33

SPARK FIRE WITH A KNIFE

Use a high-carbon steel blade or scrounge up an axe head or steel file; stainless steel blades won't work. Find a hunk of hard stone. Besides flint, quartz, quartzite, and chert work well. The trick is to stay away from round rocks; you need one with a ridge sharp enough to peel minuscule slivers of metal from the steel. When they catch fire from friction, that's what causes the spark. Add highly flammable tinder. Start sparking.

STEP 1 Hold the stone with the sharp ridge on a horizontal plane extending from your hand. Depending on where the sparks land, hold a piece of char cloth, tinder fungus, dry grass bundle, or Vaseline-soaked cotton ball under your thumb and on top of the rock or set the fire-starting material on the ground.

STEP 2 If you're using a fixed-blade knife or axe head, wrap the sharp edge with a piece of leather or cloth. With the back of the blade, strike the stone with a glancing, vertical blow. If the tinder is on the ground, aim the sparks down toward it.

STEP 3 Gently blow any embers or coals into a flame.

Flint and knife blade

Flint and file

Flint and axe head

34 BUILD A FIRE IN THE RAIN

There are those who can and those who think they can. Here's how to be one of those who really can.

STEP 1 Allow three times as much time for fire building as you'd need in dry conditions.

STEP 2 Dry tinder may be under rocks, ledges, and logs and in tree hollows. The underside of leaning deadfalls can be dry in a downpour; chop out chunks of good wood. Conifer stumps hold flammable resins.

STEP 3 Look up. Search for dry kindling and fuel off the wet ground. Fallen branches that are suspended in smaller trees will likely be rot-free. Locate a dense conifer and harvest the low, dead twigs and branches that die off as the tree grows. Shred the bark with your fingers.

STEP 4 Make what you can't find. Use a knife or hatchet blade to scrape away wet wood surfaces.

As the fire sustains itself, construct a crosshatched "log cabin" of wet wood around it with a double-layered roof. The top layer of wood will deflect rain while the lower level dries.

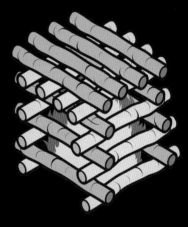

35 BUILD A FIRE ON SNOW

Go through the ice, over the bow, or into a blizzard and you'll need a fire—fast and before your fleece and fingers freeze. Let's assume you have a workable lighter. Here's how to spark an inferno no matter how much snow is on the ground.

STEP 1 Start busting brush. You'll need a two-layer fire platform of green wrist-thick (or larger) branches to raft your blaze above deep snow cover. Lay down a row of 3-foot-long branches and then another perpendicular row on top. Stay away from overhanging boughs; rising heat will melt snow trapped in foliage.

STEP 2 Lay out the fuel and don't scrimp on this step. Collect and organize plenty of dry tinder and kindling and twice as many large branches as you think you'll need. Super-dry tinder is critical. Birch bark, pine needles, wood shavings, pitch splinters, cattail fluff, and the dead, dry twigs from the sheltered lower branches of conifers are standards. Place tinder between your hands and rub vigorously to shred the material. You'll need a nest as least as large as a Ping-Pong ball. Pouring rain and snow? Think creatively: dollar bills, pocket lint, fuzzy wool, and a snipped piece of shirt fabric will work.

STEP 3 Plan the fire so it dries out wet wood as it burns. Place a large branch or dry rock across the back of the fire and arrange wet wood across the fire a few inches above the flame. Don't crisscross; laying the wood parallel will aid the drying process.

36

BOIL WATER FOR SAFE DRINKING

Without chemicals or a filtering or purifying device, the only option for disinfecting water is to bring it to a boil. But how long to simmer plain ol' H2O? Heat will kill bacteria, viruses, and parasites before the water reaches 212°F (100°C), so once the liquid is boiling—and has cooled down a bit—it's safe to drink.

But there's more to the process than simply setting a pot on a fire or stove. First, bring a small amount of water to a rapid boil, swirl it around the pot to clean the sides, and pour it out. Refill the pot and bring the fresh batch to a rolling boil. Pour a quarter cup on the ground to help sterilize the rim of the container and then fill water bottles as needed. And be sure you don't pour disinfected water back into the water bottle you used to dip the dirty stuff from the creek in the first place.

Boiling water removes much of its oxygen and gives it a flat taste, so add a drink flavoring agent or pour the water back and forth between two clean containers to aerate it as it cools.

37 CAMP WITHOUT A TENT

Most modern tent rain flies can double as tarps, but there's nothing wrong with a standard tarp as long as you pre-tie guy lines and follow this routine.

PREP AT HOME Attach two 18-inch (46 cm) guylines to each corner of the tarp. Attach 12-inch (30.5-cm) guylines to all other grommets. In the tarp's stuff sack, stash a 50-foot (15-m) length of parachute cord for a ridgeline, another 10 sections of cord cut to 20-foot (6-m) lengths for extra grommet ties, and 12 tent stakes in case there are no trees.

IN THE FIELD Once you're out in the woods, all your prep pays off. To create your lean-to-style shelter, start by tying a ridgeline to two trees. To attach the tarp, wrap one corner guyline clockwise a half-dozen times around the ridgeline and wind its mate counterclockwise a half-dozen times in the opposite direction. Connect them with a shoelace knot. Stretch the tarp out and repeat on the opposite corner. Tie the remaining guylines along this edge to the ridgeline. Stake out the back and sides. Erect a center pole to peak the tarp so the rain runs off.

38

HANG FOOD FROM A TREE

STEP 1 Tie one end of a 40-foot (12-m) length of parachute cord to the drawcord of a small stuff sack. Tie a loop in other end of the cord; clip a small carabiner to it. Fill sack with rocks and throw over a branch at least 15 feet (4.5 m) off the ground (a). Dump rocks from sack.

STEP 2 Clip the carabiner to the drawcord of your food storage bag, as shown in the illustration below (b). Run the sack end of the cord through the carabiner and then pull on this end to snug the food bag against the bottom of the branch.

STEP 3 Find a sturdy twig and, reaching as high as possible, tie a clove hitch around it. Stand on a rock for additional height. Slowly release the rock-sack end of the rope (c). The twig will catch on the carabiner to keep the food bag hanging (d).

STEP 4 To retrieve your food, pull the rope down, remove the twig, and lower the bag.

39 CREATE SHELTER WITH A TARP

If you have two utility tarps with grommeted edges, you can create the Taj Mahal of shelters anywhere.

STEP 1 Look for four trees in a rectangle and a fifth located between two of the others on the short side.

STEP 2 Tie a tarp between the four trees. The back edge should be 3 feet (1 m) off the ground, with the forward edge as high as you can reach.

STEP 3 Tie the upper tarp in place. Position it so it slides under the forward edge of the lower tarp by a couple of feet. Once it's in place, tie the side grommets together to create an open flap in the middle of the two tarps.

STEP 4 Tie a guyline from the middle of the back edge of the lower tarp to the fifth tree to create a smoke vent.

STEP 5 Build a fire with a stacked-log back wall. Smoke will rise to the tarp roof and exit through the vent.

40 BE A MODERN CAVEMAN

There's a reason bears and other beasts hole up in caves: Caves are ready-made shelters that provide immediate protection from rain, snow, wind, or brutal sun. No need to work at erecting a hut—just move in and set up housekeeping.

WATCH OUT FOR WATER Make sure the cavern is high enough to be out of danger from flash floods, incoming tides, and storm surges.

PUT UP A FENCE Erect a low stone wall across the opening to help keep dirt from blowing around.

START A FIRE Stone walls make good reflectors for a campfire, and there's no worry of the fire spreading to nearby vegetation and getting out of control. To keep campfire smoke from becoming a problem, build the fire near the cave entrance.

BEAT THE DRAFT Because they are made of rock, caves generally retain the cold. They're good places to escape the heat of a hot desert, but not so desirable in the dead of winter. Unless you can get a good fire going or partition a section of the cavern into a small room, cold air will always surround you.

41 BREAK BIGGER BRANCHES

No axe, no saw, and here comes the bitter cold. In such a situation, knowing what to do can mean the difference between a cozy bivvy and a frigid one. The trick is to break limbs of dead and downed trees into usable 18-inch (46-cm) sections. When you need heartier fuel than what you can render by breaking a few branches across your knee, turn to these useful methods.

FIRE GIRDLE You can use your campfire to help you by digging a small trench radiating outward from the fire, then scraping hot coals into the trench to fill it. Place larger branches across the coals and rotate them. Once they are partially burned through, they will be easy to break.

TREE-CROTCH LEVER Find a sturdy tree crotch about waist high. Insert a dead tree branch into the crotch and push or pull the ends until the wood breaks. This is the quickest way to render dead branches up to 20 feet (6 m) long into campfire-size chunks.

KNIFE NOTCH Cut a V-notch into one side of a branch, lean it against a tree trunk or place one end on top of a rock, and kick the branch at the notch.

TWO-MAN PUSH-PULL Two men can break a long branch into pieces by centering the branch on a sturdy tree and pushing or pulling against opposite ends.

42 BUTCHER A WET LOG

Forget searching for tinder fungus and belly-button lint to start your fire. With a hatchet, you can render fire-starting scrap from a wet log.

STEP 1 Find a solid log no more than 10 inches (25 cm) in diameter. Coniferous wood like pine or cedar works best due to its flammable resin. Cut a 12-inch (30.5-cm) section from the log.

STEP 2 Split the log into quarters. Lay one quarter on the ground, bark side down. Score the edge with two 1-inch-deep cuts, 4 inches (10 cm) apart (a). Shave thin 4-inch-long dry wood curls and splinters (b). Pound these curls with the back of the hatchet to break up the wood fibers and then rub some of these between your palms to separate the fibers further. This is your tinder; you'll need two handfuls.

STEP 3 Split pencil-size pieces from the wedge corners of a remaining quarter. Break these into 6-inch (15 cm) pieces for kindling.

STEP 4 Continue to split the quarters, utilizing the innermost and driest pieces. Use these as small and large pieces of fuel.

43 SPLIT A LOG WITH A KNIFE

A knife is no replacement for an axe when it comes to rendering firewood. Still, you can use a hunting knife to expose the dry interior of a damp log by pounding the back of the blade with a wood baton.

Make several shingles this way, splitting thin, U-shaped wooden slices from the side of a round of firewood. Angle the edges of the shingles to make wedges and then insert the wedges into an existing lengthwise crack in a log. (If there isn't one, create one with your blade.) Hammer the wedges with a wood baton to split the log end-to-end and expose more surface for burning.

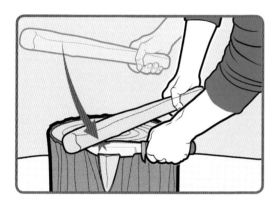
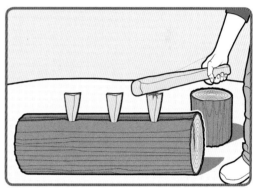

44 SPLIT LOGS THE SMART WAY

Splitting firewood doesn't require the strength of an ogre. But whale away without a plan, and you will generate more body heat than campfire BTUs.

FORGET THE AXE Use a 6- to 8-pound (2.7- to 3.6-kg) maul, erring on the light side—velocity matters more than mass. Dulling the edge slightly prevents it from sticking in the wood. Set up a chopping block. Get a hard surface under the log. Otherwise, the ground will absorb the blow.

THINK BEFORE YOU STRIKE Look for splits that extend from the center outward, or other cracks in the end grain. Exploit these splits or cracks first. Otherwise aim your first blows toward the barked edge of the round. It's easier to extract the blade if it's on the edge. Use your next blows to walk the split across the round.

AIM LOW Strike with the maul as if the first 3 or 4 inches (8 to 10 cm) of wood don't exist. Visualize the maul moving all the way through each piece of wood—and be sure every swing counts.

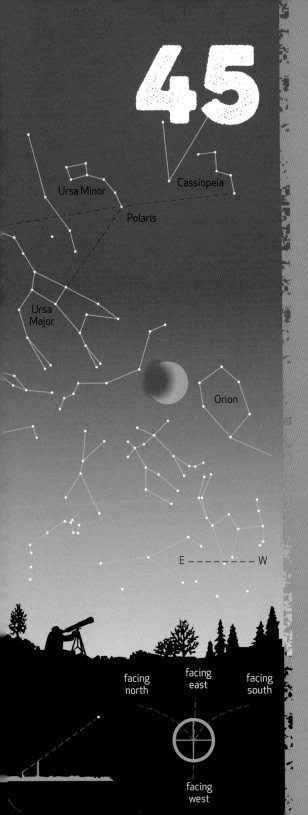

NAVIGATE BY THE NIGHT SKY

The lost have turned their eyes upward for direction since long before man slew his first mammoth. Here is how the moon and stars can help you find your way home.

NORTH BY NORTH STAR Polaris is the only star in the Northern Hemisphere that doesn't travel. It always points within 2 degrees of true north, making orientation simple. Locate the pointer stars on the bucket of the Big Dipper in Ursa Major. Observe the spacing between the two stars and then follow their direction five equal spaces to Polaris. You can also fix the position of Polaris, which is not a particularly bright star, using Cassiopeia.

DIRECTIONS BY MOONLIGHT By noting when the moon rises, it's simple to tell east from west. When the moon rises before midnight, the illuminated side faces west. If it rises after midnight, the illuminated side faces east.

LET THE HUNTER BE YOUR GUIDE During hunting season in the Northern Hemisphere, Orion can be found patrolling the southern horizon. This one is easy to spot because Orion rises due east and sets due west and the three horizontal stars that form his belt line up on an east-west line.

SIGHT ON A STAR You can roughly calculate direction by noting the path of a star's travel (with the exception of Polaris, all stars rise in the east and set in the west). Face a star and drive a stick into the ground. Next back up 10 feet and drive in a second stick so that the two sticks line up pointing toward the star. If the star seems to fall after a few minutes, you are facing west; if it rises, you are facing east; if it curves to the right, you are facing south; if it curves to the left, you are facing north.

46

SEE IN THE DARK

If you've ever wished that you could see in the dark, you're in luck! With these simple steps, you'll soon be able to maneuver in low-light conditions.

PROTECT In the critical minutes of dawn and dusk, shield your eyes from the sun. When moving your field of vision, allow your eyes to travel below the horizon line or shut your eyes as you move them. Before dawn, use the least amount of light required for the task; a low-level red or green light is best. Practice walking at night to increase your comfort level and clear favorite trails so you won't need a flashlight.

BOOST Use peripheral vision by focusing to the side of an object. Scan when you can; when your eyes linger on a particular object, they will adapt to whatever light is available. Try to get lower than the target to see the object's contours better.

47 STOP BLEEDING

No one likes to see blood coming out of somebody's body—least of all his or her own. But don't just cover it up: It's pressure that stops the bleeding. Here's how to squeeze off the flow.

STEP 1 Find the source of the bleeding. Got multiple cuts? Deal with the worst first and then tend to the lesser ones.

STEP 2 Place a sterile compress directly over the wound and apply firm pressure. Don't be afraid to push hard. If the cut is on an extremity, place pressure on both sides of the limb so that it doesn't bend back and away from the pressure.

STEP 3 If the compress soaks through, don't remove it. Simply add another compress on top of the first and continue with the pressure. Keep stacking bandages one on top of another until the bleeding has stopped.

STEP 4 Remove the compresses and flush the wound with water to clean.

48 DISINFECT A WOUND

Knowing how to disinfect a wound can be critical. Even small cuts can become infected—especially when you're out in the wilderness, which is not renowned for its sterility. And when your body is fighting off an infection, it's diverting valuable resources away from your overall health, leaving you susceptible to other illnesses and complications.

STEP 1 Stop the bleeding and assess the injury. If the bleeding won't stop, or if the wound is deep and you can tell it'll need stitches, seek medical attention. If you're going to the hospital, don't bother with cleaning a severe wound. Leave it to a pro.

STEP 2 Flush the wound with clean water. There's no need to use hydrogen peroxide; the burning sensation doesn't mean the wound is getting cleaner—it just plain smarts.

STEP 3 Saturate the wound with a triple antibiotic ointment before applying a dressing to keep out dirt and debris.

49 DEAL WITH BLOOD LOSS

When you're in the outdoors, many objects you encounter will be pointed, jagged, or razor-sharp. Human flesh doesn't stand a chance against a misdirected axe or an errant blade, and that doesn't take into account accidents involving sharp rocks or a skin-shredding tumble on a trail. So it's little surprise that blood-loss injuries are the most common afflictions in outdoor situations. Here are four common categories of bleeding and what to do for each.

OOZE An abrasion or common scrape tears open capillaries, resulting in a slow trickle of blood from the wound. Infection is your biggest threat here.
- Disinfect the wound.
- Use moderate pressure to stop the bleeding.
- Keep the wound moist with aloe vera or antibiotic ointment until it heals.
- Cover it with a semipermeable dressing.
- Change the dressing daily and inspect the wound for infection, which might require professional treatment.

FLOW If dark red blood gushes steadily, a vein has been opened. You've got to clean the wound and stop the flow until you can get the victim to a hospital.
- Elevate the injury above the heart.
- Use tweezers to remove any debris that is lodged in the cut. Disinfect the wound.
- Apply direct pressure to the injury. You can apply pressure with bare hands at first, but then search for something to serve as a direct-pressure pad.
- After the bleeding stops, use tape or cloth strips to secure the dressing over the wound.

SPURT If bright red blood shoots from the wound, you have arterial bleeding, and it's highly dangerous. Forget disinfecting; just stop the bleeding.
- Elevate the injury above the heart.
- Aggressively apply pressure.
- If the bleeding doesn't stop and the wound is on a limb, tie a tourniquet above the wound and tighten it until the blood stops flowing. Be warned, however, that tourniquets themselves are dangerous. Use one only when you must.
- Call 911 or transport the victim to a medical facility immediately.

INTERNAL If someone has been in a high-speed automobile accident or if a sharp object hit near an organ, he or she may be bleeding on the inside.
- Monitor for hypovolemia (a state in which blood levels are drastically reduced). Shock, pallor, rapid breathing, confusion, and lack of urine are all signs.
- Incline the victim toward the injured side. This constrains the blood flow to the damaged area.
- Stabilize the victim, treat for shock, and call 911 or transport the victim to a medical facility immediately.

50 IMMOBILIZE AN ARM INJURY

If you've injured one (with a fracture, severe sprain, or especially gnarly cut), you'll need to immobilize it for a while. Fashioning a sling is pretty straightforward, but it's a core bit of knowledge to have at your disposal; in particular, use this method if you're out in the wild and away from medical care.

STEP 1 Start with a square cloth approximately 3 by 3 feet (1 m by 1 m). Lay the cloth out flat, then fold it once diagonally to make a triangle.

STEP 2 Slip the injured arm into the fold and bring both ends up around the neck, slanting the forearm up slightly.

STEP 3 Tie the corners in a knot. Gravity will naturally pull the forearm back to parallel position.

STEP 4 Use a belt to immobilize the arm against the body. Wrap it around the chest, above the forearm, and then cinch it closed but not too tightly. Circulation is key.

 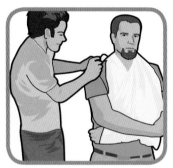 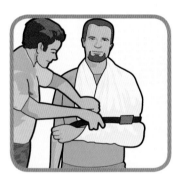

51 BANDAGE A WOUND

It takes 72 hours for skin to close up and become airtight. For small cuts and scrapes, just keep the area clean. For large cuts, you may need to do a bit more.

DON'T STITCH IT UP We've all seen action heroes use a needle and thread. Unless you have sterile sutures, a suture needle, and a tool to get it through the skin, this option isn't happening. (Likewise, leave sterilizing and closing a wound with a hot knife blade to the movie stars.)

BUTTERFLY IT The best way to close a wound is to apply sterile adhesive strips after disinfecting it. First, line up the edges of the cut. Then, starting in the center of the wound, place the end of an adhesive strip on one side of the cut. As you lay the strip across the wound, push the wound's edges together. Apply these bandages in a crisscross pattern the length of the cut to keep the sides in contact; dress with a sterile wrap.

BE SUPER In a pinch, superglue can hold your skin closed—it worked for soldiers in the Vietnam War. Just make sure you coat only the outside edges of the cut, not in the cut itself.

52

TREAT
FOR SHOCK

During trauma, the circulatory system diverts the body's blood supply to vital internal organs. This redistribution of oxygen can ultimately lead to shock, which is fatal if not treated properly. Pain and fear both contribute to shock, compounding the danger from the injury.

STEP 1 Recognize the symptoms of shock, such as rapid pulse, gray or pale skin (especially around the lips), and cold, clammy skin on which the sweat doesn't evaporate. Other symptoms of shock, such as gasping for air, nausea, and vomiting, can occur as the condition worsens. At this point it is crucial to proceed carefully with the next steps.

STEP 2 Have the victim lie down, keeping his or her head low. Treat any outward injuries, such as bleeding.

STEP 3 Elevate the victim's feet slightly, carefully avoiding any injuries to the legs.

STEP 4 Loosen restrictive clothing, such as belts—it'll help the victim breathe more freely.

STEP 5 Keep the victim warm with blankets or coats.

STEP 6 Talk to focus the victim's mind and reassure him or her that all will be well.

53 FAKE A SLING

No sling? No problem. When it comes to immobilizing an arm, just about any kind of cloth or material can work, so look around. For instance, you can place a loop of rope or a belt loosely around the neck, slide the arm inside so the wrist rests in the loop, knot or cinch the rope or belt in place and there you go: The arm is unlikely to bounce and incur further injury.

But let's say you're out on a hike without any rope, and—on today of all days—you're sporting pants with an elastic waistband. Try unbuttoning a few buttons in the center of your shirt and putting your hand through the hole. Place your hand under the strap of your backpack. A pair of pants also makes for an easy tie—just use the crotch of the jeans to support the arm and knot the legs behind the neck. Sure, you may be the guy in the woods with your pants off, but if your arm's broken, you've got bigger problems to worry about.

54 SET A BONE

If you've ever heard the grim sound of a bone breaking, you know just how dire this situation can be. Getting to a hospital is always the best recourse, but if that's not possible and blood isn't circulating to the limb, setting the bone might be the only way to save the arm or leg. Here's how.

STEP 1 Many breaks don't need setting, but transverse, oblique, or impacted fractures might. If bone is protruding, don't set it. Just immobilize it.

STEP 2 Press on the skin below the fracture site. It should turn white and then quickly return to pink. Pale or bluish skin, numbness, tingling, or the lack of a pulse in the limb indicates a loss of circulation.

STEP 3 To reduce swelling, pain, and damage to the tissues, realign the limb by pulling in opposite directions on both sides of the break.

STEP 4 Use a splint to keep the break stable.

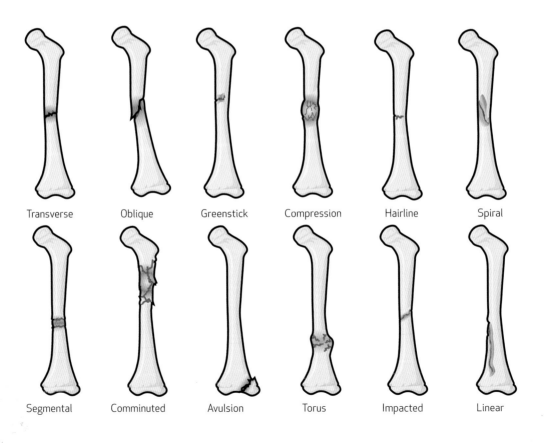

Transverse   Oblique   Greenstick   Compression   Hairline   Spiral

Segmental   Comminuted   Avulsion   Torus   Impacted   Linear

55

IDENTIFY AND TREAT BURNS

Skin is the body's largest organ, and it's made up of three layers of varying thicknesses. The severity of a burn depends on how deep it penetrates, and the treatment varies for each type of burn.

FIRST DEGREE These minor burns can be caused by anything from hot liquids to sun exposure. They heal on their own, but it's a good idea to apply a cool compress or aloe vera gel. Anti-inflammatory drugs will hasten healing.

SECOND DEGREE Flame flashes, hot metals, and boiling liquids cause this burn, which usually penetrates the skin's second layer. You'll know if you've got one because blisters will form, and it takes longer than a few days to heal. Usually it's enough to flood the site with cool water and trim away any loose skin (but leave the blisters intact to prevent infection). A daily slather of aloe vera and a nonadhesive dressing are also recommended. The exception? If the burn is larger than 3 inches (7.5 cm) in diameter, or if the burn is on the victim's face, hands, feet, groin, or bottom, it's best to go to an emergency room for care.

THIRD DEGREE This full-thickness burn is very severe. It reaches through all three layers of the skin. In the event of a third-degree burn, treat the victim for shock and transport him or her to a hospital. Skin grafts are always required.

FOURTH DEGREE Another full-thickness burn, the fourth-degree burn damages structures below the skin, such as ligaments and tendons. These burns are bad news: They destroy nerves, so the victim won't feel anything. Amputation and permanent disability are likely, so your best bet is to evacuate the victim to a medical facility as soon as humanly possible.

56 MAKE A SPLINT

If someone injures a leg in the wild, immobilization is key—but you still have to walk back to civilization, so staying still isn't an option. Set the bone and craft a splint with a sleeping pad, a piece of cardboard, or other flexible material.

STEP 1 Stop any bleeding with direct pressure.

STEP 2 Check for a pulse below the fracture and look at the skin—if it's pale, circulation may be cut off.

STEP 3 Slide the unfolded splint material beneath the limb and pad it for comfort and stability.

STEP 4 Fold the splint around the leg, securing the splint with elastic, gauze, or other material. Get the level of the compression just right: The splint should be just tight enough to prevent the bone from shifting, but not so tight that it impedes circulation. If the break involves a joint, secure the splint both above and below it for extra stability.

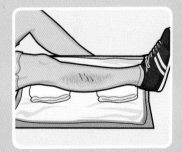

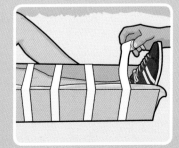

57 USE SUPERGLUE TO CLOSE A WOUND

So-called "superglues" were used in the Vietnam War to close wounds and stem bleeding. Dermabond is a medical formulation that minimizes irritation; but as many an outdoorsman will attest, plain ol' superglue will hold a cut together better than a strip bandage, and instances of irritation are rare. If you're stuck in the backcountry with no other way to close a wound, this will get you through until you can get to a doctor. Always use an unopened tube. Clean the cut and pinch shut. Dab a drop or two of glue directly on the incision, then spread along the length of the cut with something clean. The bandage is watertight and seals out infecting agents.

58 MAKE A FIRE BED

It's cold enough to freeze whiskey, and you're stuck in the woods sans a sleeping bag? Make like a pot roast and construct a life-saving fire bed. Scrape out a gravelike trench in the dirt about 1 foot (30.5 cm) wide and 8 inches (20 cm) deep. Line it with very dry egg-size to fist-size stones, if available. (Wet rocks from a stream or lake can explode when heated.)

Next, burn a hot fire into coals and spread a layer in the trench. Cover with at least 4 inches of dirt and tamp down with your boot. Wait one hour. If the ground warms in less than an hour, add more dirt. Now spread out a ground sheet of canvas, plastic, or spare clothing. Check the area twice for loose coals that could ignite your makeshift mattress. Ease onto your fire bed and snooze away.

CONQUER ALTITUDE SICKNESS

The cause is simple: going too high too fast. And the higher the altitude, the longer it takes to acclimate. So when you're climbing in the mountains, slow down. Ascending beyond 8,000 feet (2,438 m) should be done at a rate of no more than 1,000 feet (304 m) per day. Avoid strenuous exertion for at least 24 hours after reaching new heights and increase water intake as you go.

And if you don't follow these instructions?

Watch for signs of two forms of serious altitude sickness: high-altitude pulmonary edema (HAPE)—characterized by breathlessness, fatigue, dry cough, and blue lips and nails—and high-altitude cerebral edema (HACE), which typically features a severe headache, loss of coordination, and confusion. Both are potentially deadly. Victims must immediately descend at least 2,000 feet (600 m) to save their lives, and then they must be evacuated to a medical facility as soon as possible.

YOU DID IT ALL RIGHT. NOW WHAT?

Despite your preparation—studying the area, packing like a pro, and having a well-honed set of skills and tools—you find yourself in unfamiliar territory with no idea how to get out of it. It could happen to anyone. Maybe you got injured or sick, bad weather moved in—or you just took a wrong turn. How it happened doesn't matter. What matters now is staying strong until you can walk out of the woods on your own two feet. This chapter gives you all the information you need to access the essential elements of staying alive—food, water, and shelter—in the wilderness. Getting lost in the woods is no joke—but believe us, knowing how to fish with your shirt or filter water with your pants could save your life.

60 SURVIVE FOR THREE DAYS

Could you make it on your own in the woods for three days? With the wild-food knowledge you've gained so far, you're well on your way. But there's more to surviving than just staying fed. Here's what else to consider:

Make sure you understand the survival priorities: shelter, water, fire, and food. You also need to know how to find your way back to civilization—or signal for help if you're unable to move. You'll need to maintain your morale, take care of any injuries, and stay safe from harm.

No matter how your wilderness trial (or, to put a positive spin on it, adventure) unfolds, you will need the skills to turn nothing into something. Follow these priorities of survival as we work our way through an outdoor excursion gone wrong.

GET SHELTER

Your top survival priority the instant you realize you're lost is shelter. Use the space blanket from your survival kit to stay warm or turn the trash bag into a sleeping bag by filling it with leaves. Build a small (barely bigger than your body) insulated "nest" from materials like sticks, grass, and leaves. If your clothes are inadequate, stuff them with leaves, grasses, or any other material that can trap your body heat.

FIND A DRINK

You'll need to source some water on the first day, too. Lay a trash bag in a hole to catch water from precipitation and look for natural springs—a common way to get reasonably safe drinking water without any tools or materials. Don't drink any water without disinfecting it—use your kit's metal container to boil it or look for bottles and cans that can be used as boiling vessels.

START A FIRE

By the end of the first day, that fire-starting gear in your survival kit will be worth its weight in gold. But many fire-starting methods can be inadequate in wet or windy weather, so be sure your kit is stocked with some tinder or fuel. Cotton balls, dryer lint, curls of birch bark, and even greasy snacks can help build the flame. Fire is also a dependable way to signal for help.

SCROUNGE A MEAL

You'll spend most of the second and third days looking for food—when you're not signaling for help. If you're unsure about the edible plants, stick to animal foods. Freshwater fish, worms, crickets, and other critters are safe to eat—just cook them thoroughly, in case they have parasites or pathogens. Stay strong and focus on calorie-dense foods like fatty animals, tree nuts, and organ meats.

KEEP IT POSITIVE

A positive attitude and a generous streak of mental toughness can be literal lifesavers, especially under dire circumstances. The nights are usually the worst time during emergencies: It's just you and your thoughts. Find little ways to maintain your morale and remain motivated to survive. Think of family, friends, and loved ones and fight to stay alive—not just for yourself but for them.

SIGNAL FOR HELP

The skill of signaling is your ticket home. The whistle from your survival kit can signal your distress to others, day or night, as long as you have breath to blow it; and a mirror can give you a signal range much farther than the sound of the whistle can carry. Don't forget about the power of a smoky fire, either.

STAY SAFE

You may face dangers in the wilderness, so arm yourself for survival as best you can. Carry a spear, club, knife, or whatever you can find in case you need to defend yourself. Consider all of the sources of harm that could befall you and make plans to avoid becoming one of their victims.

START WITH AN ADVANTAGE

NEVER LEAVE HOME WITHOUT IT A survival kit should be part of your gear no matter what you're doing outside. Pack the following items in a kit and keep it close.

- ☐ A space blanket and a large garbage bag for shelter and catching rain
- ☐ A metal cup or bowl to boil water for disinfection
- ☐ Signal gear: a whistle for an audible signal day or night; a mirror for a visual signal on sunny days
- ☐ A compass to help you find your way and guide you in a straight line
- ☐ Multiple fire starters: a lighter, waterproof matches, and a ferrocerium rod are good choices
- ☐ First-aid gear: a small medical pack can come in very handy

61 BLAZE A TRAIL

Not certain you can find your way back if you head out into the wild? It can be a big problem in snowy conditions and featureless terrain. If you're short on navigational equipment but you're a crafty survivor, you can mark your own path and make it back to camp without any hassle. Use these techniques to blaze a trail across any landscape.

MAKE MARKS As you traverse forests or fields, mark your travel on prominent trees and rocks. During emergencies, high-impact marking (like chopping arrows into tree bark or chipping rock) may be a necessary method. For lower levels of distress, a simple piece of black charcoal from your campfire can be used as a pencil; draw arrows or write messages on trees, rocks, and other surfaces to mark your progress. These markings can last for months, but will eventually wear away. Always make your marks at eye level for easy recognition.

BUILD A CAIRN In rocky country, pillars of stone known as cairns are used as landmarks and waypoints. Build your own if time and energy allow or construct a simpler version—a snowman or a cone of tall sticks. Place these in open areas to indicate the trail at a distance or to signal other information. Similarly, you can make arrows and other signs for pathfinding on the ground— but know they'll be easily buried under a light snow.

TIE FLAGS Small strips of colorful fabric or material can be used as excellent trail markers in brushy areas and woodland terrain. Plastic survey tape is my favorite to carry. Choose bright colors that are not found in nature, like hot pink or neon purple or orange, for the best visibility. Hang small strips of the tape at eye level, within view of the last marker, and your trail will be established.

62 TRACK YOURSELF

Following your own tracks (or someone else's) falls into the fascinating realm of man tracking. This age-old art form is easy in snowy environments, and it can provide you with a viable way of getting back to camp. Follow these steps to find your own tracks and follow them back to familiar stomping grounds.

STEP 1 Move quickly! Whether you are following tracks through mounting snowfall or melting frost, move quickly for the best chance of keeping up with the disappearing trail.

STEP 2 Pay attention to your stride and gait. Depending on your height, footwear, injuries, the substrate you're walking on, and other factors, your tracks and trail should have some repeating patterns. Study the measurements of your feet, the distance and width between your footprints, and any other distinctive details.

STEP 3 Use these measurements to find any lost tracks—you'll be able to make an educated guess as to where the next set should be. You can also pick up your trail by looking for aerial signs, like broken twigs or places with knocked-down snow.

63

AVOID GETTING LOST

Hey, we've all strayed off a trail or two, but losing your way when you're far from civilization is one of the foremost ways to wind up in deep trouble. Fortunately, getting lost is easily preventable.

STEP 1 Get a map of the area in which you'll be traveling and study it before your trip.

STEP 2 Use the map and a compass or GPS while you're there, constantly staying aware of your position.

STEP 3 Keep a map in your mind, too. Imagine what the terrain would look like from a bird's-eye view and visualize your place in that terrain. Think of that little "You Are Here" arrow on the big map at the trailhead and keep it updated in your mind.

STEP 4 Take mental note of prominent topographical features such as mountain peaks or bluffs, valleys, rivers and lakes and keep them in view as much as possible.

STEP 5 Look back frequently and remember the landmarks behind you—especially if you'll be returning in that direction.

STEP 6 When venturing off the trails, use a compass or distant features like mountains or canyons to help you travel in straight lines.

STEP 7 Always make sure somebody responsible knows where you're going and exactly when you're supposed to be coming back.

64 ASSESS YOUR SITUATION

It's decision time: Do you stay or go? If you're stuck at a campsite or next to a failed vehicle, you can wait until help arrives—or you can try hiking back to civilization. Assuming you're healthy, here's your checklist for sitting tight or getting going.

STAY IF

- ☐ The campsite or vehicle is intact. It's a ready-made shelter—leave it only as a last resort.
- ☐ Your camp or vehicle has ample food and water.
- ☐ You need to conserve energy because you lack supplies or are injured.
- ☐ The site or vehicle is visible to searchers.

HIKE OUT IF

- ☐ You're certain nobody is looking for you.
- ☐ You're sure of which way to go and how long it will take to reach help.
- ☐ You've got a well-stocked wilderness survival kit that you can carry. If you don't, you shouldn't be in the wilderness in the first place, should you?

65 MEASURE REMAINING DAYLIGHT

Setting up camp in the dark is no picnic. To help you decide whether you're better off continuing to hike or stopping to set up camp, estimate how much time is left until sundown. Hold your hand at arm's length with your fingers positioned horizontally between the horizon and the sun. The width of each finger between the sun and the horizon is roughly equal to 15 minutes before sunset.

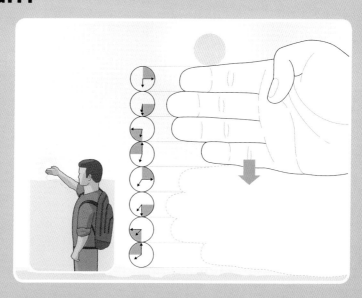

66 SURVIVE MENTALLY

The art of survival begins not when you set up camp, but as soon as you address your mental survival game. The mental elements you need to make it through an emergency are so important, in fact, that I either begin or end most of my classes with this topic. And thanks to your ancestors, you already possess these amazing survival tools.

ATTITUDE "Positive mental attitude" can be found in every survival book, Scout manual, and wilderness class, but don't discount it as cliché or lip service—PMA is a real necessity, and may be one of the most important (and hardest) skills to master.

MENTAL TOUGHNESS I'm not talking about how much stamina or how many calluses you have. This is the strength of your will and the toughness of your mind. To be mentally tough, you must tolerate the intolerable, suffer through the insufferable, and overpower your own weakness and inclination to give up or give in.

MOTIVATION What motivates a person to stay alive, maintaining hope and endurance, when everything has gone wrong? Many survival stories involve the survivor's devotion to a higher power or their intense desire to get back to loved ones. And a few have even credited their burning desire for revenge.

WORK ETHIC A major player in survival, your work ethic can be built up over time, just like any other skill. A survivor sticks with the job until the job gets done, and a strong work ethic can go a long way toward making up for the things that luck doesn't provide.

ADAPTABILITY The ability to adapt and the ability to survive have always been closely related. Think about plants and animals: Those that cannot adapt to a changing environment die out, while the ones that adapt and change are the survivors. Learn to adapt to shifting situations and to recognize what's worth continuing versus what needs to be abandoned for the greater good.

67 AVOID THESE PITFALLS

The human animal is a complex thing, and it's important to acknowledge the natural traits that can hinder our survival and maybe even cost us our lives in a survival situation. Don't leave these tendencies unchecked.

PREVENT PANIC Unrestrained fear is one of your worst enemies, and it can directly lead to making bad decisions, lost time, and wasted energy. Don't let fear get the better of you! Focus on small but productive tasks and keep your wild imagination under control. That rustling you hear in the bush won't always be a bear—just sometimes.

FIGHT PESSIMISM The opposite of PMA, a dyed-in-the-wool pessimist's fatalistic attitude can leave you feeling overwhelmed and helpless. Suck it up and try to stay as positive as you can while maintaining a grip on the reality of the situation.

BOYCOTT LAZINESS It's hard work building survival shelters, hauling water, and carrying firewood. Survival is not a vacation. Being lazy and seeking the easiest path will eventually cause you some serious trouble. You need to honestly look at your workload, pad it a little for some extra security, and then get it done.

SAY GOODBYE TO STUBBORNNESS Stubbornness, though occasionally used for the greater good, is a refusal to adapt. It's very simple to identify, but harder to treat. Don't keep throwing lit matches into a poorly constructed fire lay; you did it wrong and you need to rebuild. Try something else rather than blindly continuing on a path that's not working out.

ELIMINATE IGNORANCE Despite the wealth of information available today, there are a lot of people who couldn't survive their way out of a paper bag. In short, don't let other people get you killed. Many people think survival looks easy, and they overestimate their ability to do anything physical. You need to know what to do, how to do it, and you need to have successfully practiced the skill before. Practice these skills when you don't necessarily need them. With experience comes wisdom.

68

PLAN YOUR PRIORITIES

We begin with the survival priorities. These are the tasks to accomplish and the issues to tackle, organized from the most pressing items to the lesser concerns. This is your game plan for success—don't ignore it or mix up the list on a whim. Follow these steps in order.

MAKE SHELTER Your clothing is your first line of shelter, and each layer of insulation counts. Seek shelter from the cold as best you can. You don't need tools to build small insulated nests of natural materials or cast-off items. Think of the nests you have seen in nature and create one that you can just barely squeeze into.

CARE FOR YOUR WOUNDS A solid first-aid kit should always be part of your survival gear.

Medical aid should be rendered after shelter is secured, unless the injury is more life-threatening than exposure. Even without a kit, you can use pressure points to slow bleeding, and treat ailments like hypothermia and dehydration.

FIND WATER Melting snow and finding a natural spring are two safe ways to get drinking water without much in the way of tools and materials. What you don't want to do is emulate the TV survival gurus who demonstrate drinking out of puddles and waterways without disinfecting the water. This is the fast track to dysentery, which can kill a healthy person when left untreated. And don't eat snow for hydration. If it's cold enough for snow, it's cold enough for hypothermia.

CREATE A FIRE Lighting a fire can be a monumental task, or even an unachievable task, in cold, wet conditions. Considering fire's myriad uses—water boiling, heating, lighting, signaling, and cooking—you should always carry fire-building implements and backup fuel sources.

SCROUNGE A MEAL Foraging for food can be a pleasant experience that yields delicious results—when you have lots of time, leisure, and cooking tools at your disposal. But all those gourmet sensibilities go out the window when you are scavenging to stay alive. If you don't know how to identify the local wild edible plants, stick with animal foods. Most critters are safe for human consumption, as long as you cook them thoroughly to kill parasites or pathogens.

SIGNAL FOR HELP This is your golden ticket to get home. Signaling can happen after the other survival priorities have been handled or, better still, during the procurement of your survival supplies. Signal often and in varied ways to multiply your chances of attracting help and rescue.

69 COUNT YOUR CALORIES

We've discussed the value of maintaining a survival mentality and the critical list of survival priorities. These two things are the raw material from which survival is crafted. But there is a more basic requirement that exemplifies and equates to survival: calorie count. In its basest form, survival is about mitigating calorie loss and acquiring more calories. In an emergency, you want to hold onto every calorie you can—and get more in order to sustain you going forward. Here are the two ways we can keep calories in mind during survival.

CUT YOUR LOSSES The cold can be one of the most ruthless thieves of your body's stored calories. People who become lost in a frigid landscape often suffer a fast and shocking weight loss. Even with warm bedding to sleep in and adequate clothing to wear, your body has to rewarm a lot of tissue with each breath you take. This rewarming happens through your body's efforts to ramp up your metabolism for heat, which burns a lot of

calories. Consuming bad food or water is another way to lose the calorie game. If you become ill (diarrhea, vomiting, or dysentery), you lose the calories you just consumed—and sometimes more. Stop calorie losses before they occur—work a little harder to make a nice shelter, rather than wasting calories shivering each night. Make the effort to boil your water and cook your food thoroughly to prevent illness and calorie loss. Constant losses can add up to serious shortages over time.

BE CALORIE-CONSCIOUS Try to find high-calorie wild foods if you're caught in a wilderness survival situation. Boost the calories you are consuming by adding a little oil to your food when you're snowed in. Survival is a balancing act of calorie gain and calorie expense. You have to bring in lots of calories and make sure your activities are worth the effort. Spending the afternoon chopping through frozen soil looking for worms doesn't quite pay for itself when worms are 1 calorie per gram.

70
HANDLE ANIMAL ATTACKS

If an animal decides to make you his dinner (or turn you into pulp just for the fun of it), you have to think—and move—fast. Knowing a bit about the beastly foes that might be lurking out there will help you survive.

 ANIMAL PROFILE

 METHOD OF ATTACK

 YOUR RESPONSE

THE MOOSE owns everything—that's his attitude.

- The moose is one of the most dangerous wild animals because it's huge, powerful, and deceptively fast—not to mention willing to attack anyone it deems a trespasser.
- But then, it might just decide to leave you alone—not because it's afraid of you, but because it feels like it. You never can tell.

- A moose is predictably unpredictable, so exercise great caution.
- It typically executes its attacks with front hooves and antlers.
- When it's satisfied that you no longer pose a threat, it'll likely leave you alone.

- If a moose approaches you, back away. If it charges, run! Do not stand your ground.
- If possible, get behind a substantial barrier like a tree or boulder. If you're knocked down, scramble to get away and put something between you and that crazy moose.

THE WOLF is a tireless hunter—and the ultimate opportunist.

THE MOUNTAIN LION is sneaky and powerful—and thinks you're tasty.

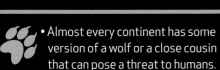

- Almost every continent has some version of a wolf or a close cousin that can pose a threat to humans.
- While attacks are rare, they do happen, especially in areas where these animals scavenge human leftovers and lose their fear of people.

- Mountain lions are among the few predators to stalk humans with the intent to eat us. Isn't that special?
- Lion encounters have grown in frequency with loss of habitat. Many lions, especially juveniles, find themselves on the fringes of development, where backyard hunting provides easy prey.

- The greatest danger of attack is during mating season, which varies depending on environment, and when females are raising their pups.
- Wolves tend to hunt in packs, surrounding their victim and wearing it down by taking turns attacking it from various angles.

- They sneak in from above and behind as you walk a trail, then pounce at an opportune moment.
- The cougar will go for your neck or throat and use sweeping attacks with its claws.
- If it takes you down, it will try to drag you into the bushes for later meals.

- When you're dealing with wolves, your response to a confrontation is key. If you try to run, they'll attack.
- If you stand your ground, face the animals, group together (if you're not alone), and approach them aggressively, the attackers will likely shy away.
- If attacked, fight back with punches and kicks to the snout.

- When faced with a cougar, do not run and do not turn your back. Either action will trigger an attack and leave you vulnerable.
- Stand your ground. Make yourself appear larger by extending your arms and waving.
- Arm yourself with a club, rock, or knife and prepare to fight.

71 READ A BEAR'S MIND

A defensive bear will appear stressed and unsure of how to act, pacing about and popping its jaws. Talk to it in a very calm voice. Don't throw anything. When it is not moving toward you, move away from it slowly and carefully. A stumble now could provoke a charge. If the bear continues to approach you, stop. Stand your ground and continue talking calmly (a). If the bear charges, use your spray or gun; wait until the last possible moment before hitting the dirt.

A predatory bear isn't intent on rendering you harmless but rather on rendering you digestible. If a bear is aware of your presence and approaches in a nondefensive, unconcerned manner, get very serious. Speak to it in a loud, firm voice. Try to get out of the bear's direction of travel but do not run. If the animal follows, stop again and make a stand (b). Shout at the bear and stare at it. Make yourself appear larger—step up on a rock or move uphill. Prepare for a charge.

72 AVOID A BEAR ATTACK

CREATE OBSTACLES When a distant bear has become aware of your presence, circle upwind to give it your scent so it can identify you as a human. Gain high ground and place objects, like a jumble of logs, between you and the bear. Back slowly away.

DRAW YOUR WEAPON At 50 to 70 to yards (46 to 64 m), a surprised bear may show aggression. Draw your pepper spray and remove the trigger guard. Talk in low tones, avoid eye contact, and back slowly away. If the bear follows, drop your pack to distract it. Climb a tree if possible.

SPRAY AND PRAY If the bear persists, give it a 1-second burst of spray at 40 feet (12 m). If the bear gets closer or charges, spray another 1-second burst at 15 feet (5 m). At 8 feet (2.5 m), empty the canister into the bear's face.

73 KNOW YOUR BEARS

All bears are scary—but some are scarier than others. Knowing which kind you're dealing with helps you figure out just how much trouble you're in.

GRIZZLY These huge beasts can weigh 800 pounds (360 kg) and stand 7 feet (more than 2 m) tall on their hind legs. They have brown fur and a distinctive hump at their shoulders, and their faces feature a dip between forehead and nose, as well as small, rounded ears. The true danger with grizzlies arises if you surprise one, or encounter a mother and cub. Do not run as that action will likely trigger an attack. Instead, back away slowly. If this huge bear charges you, your best bet is to play dead.

BLACK BEAR Despite their name, black bears' fur ranges from blond to brown to deep black. Their faces are straight from forehead to nose, and their ears are long and pointed. Adult black bears average 300 pounds (135 kg) and stand about 5 feet (1.5 m) tall when upright. This bear will come into camp and attack humans, but don't run: Face the bear and make yourself appear larger by waving your arms high. Fight for your life with sticks, rocks, or a knife.

74 FACE DOWN A BLACK BEAR

Not all bears will deliver a cute public service message like Smokey Bear, and knowing what to do when one wants to make you his lunch could save your life. Black bears are prominent across Canada and account for the majority of bear attacks on our continent. Handling one is much different than fending off a grizzly.

Stand your ground and make yourself as big as possible by raising your arms wide above your head. Be as loud and intimidating as you can.

Don't run; that will draw the bear to chase you. And stay on the ground; black bears are better at climbing trees than humans.

Fight to the bitter end. Playing dead is not a good idea with a black bear. Punch it in the nose or boot it in the groin and inflict as much pain as possible in any way possible.

75

LIVE THROUGH A GRIZZLY ENCOUNTER

If a grizzly's mauling you, cuss yourself for getting in that fix. But do it quietly, because you're supposed to be playing dead, and corpses don't talk. The griz probably doesn't want to eat you, but you've interrupted her routine (it's most likely a female protecting cubs). And now you're going to have to pay.

TAKE YOUR MAULING The best thing you can do to avoid injury or death is to shield yourself by going face-down on the ground with your backpack (let's hope you're wearing one) protecting your back. Cover your head and neck with your hands and play dead; it's your best chance of not becoming dead for real.

KEEP QUIET Expect to be batted around, perhaps bitten a few times, and maybe clawed. Stay quiet if you can, which is a tall order when a bear has one of your body parts in her mouth.

WAIT IT OUT When the bear decides you are no longer a threat or an annoyance, she'll probably huff and wander away. Stay still until she's long gone.

76 NAVIGATE BOGS AND MUSKEG

In the West these soft-bottomed lowlands are referred to as muskeg; in the East they are often called bogs. Muskeg is a Cree term, meaning low-lying marsh. There is no easy way to travel with a vehicle or walk through muskeg. Dense stands of black spruce and willow make it difficult to navigate a straight path.

NAVIGATE CAREFULLY Muskeg and peat bogs can be almost 100 feet deep, and walking on pillowy-soft clouds of moss can be a workout. Peat has the ability to hold tremendous amounts of water, and if you break through the surface it can be a quagmire to get out. The surface is held together by vegetation and its root systems. Large-soled rubber boots act like snowshoes and give more surface area to distribute weight. Tread lightly and test each step before moving forward. Try to pick something in the distance to watch and maintain your direction of travel. Head for higher ground by watching for a ridge or tree tops that extend higher than everything else in the lowlands you're navigating.

AVOID STANDING WATER The water table is always close to the surface in a muskeg, so avoid open water at all costs. The peat and moss around open water is saturated, turning it into a soup that can swallow you up. Muskeg is made of dead plant material like moss, decaying trees, and sedges. The drier it is, the less likely the earth will give way underfoot.

DON'T GET STUCK Muskeg has been known to swallow vehicles. Well-rooted clumps of willow may be the only things to winch to, that is, if you're lucky enough to find one close by. If walking, always carry a stick and probe the ground in front of you. Identifying sink holes that will give you a soaker or, worse, swallow you past the knee can be avoided. It is always better to travel on muskeg edges and not through the center of these soggy wetlands.

77 KEEP BUGS OUT OF YOUR PANTS

Even one bug bite can be too many—especially when you're in a wet environment, where the infection risk is high and the availability of calamine lotion is low.

To keep bugs from crawling inside your sleeves and pant legs, fold under the cuffs, then tie something around them. You can use spare shoelaces or elastic blousing bands, available at military surplus stores. The Velcro® cuff straps sported by commuter cyclists everywhere are also a good bet; you can find them in bike shops. And as in so many other situations, duct tape will do the trick in a pinch.

78 AVOID DREADED TRENCH FOOT

This malady gets its name from a painful condition many soldiers experienced during World War I, when they stood in the trenches for days and weeks in cold, waterlogged, filthy boots. Gradually their feet would numb and their skin would turn red or blue. Without treatment, gangrene would set in, leading to amputation. Even today, trench foot impacts unprepared outdoorsmen. Don't be one of its victims.

Prevent the problem by wearing waterproof boots and wool socks. It's also a good idea to shed your boots and socks periodically, air out and massage your feet to promote circulation, and then put on fresh socks if you have them. Your feet will feel better and smell fresher. Best of all, you'll get to keep them.

79 REMOVE A TICK

Great. In all your wilderness survival fun, you've managed to pick up a hitchhiker. Ticks are nasty little buggers that carry diseases. The longer one stays embedded in its host (that'd be you), the greater the chances for exposure to the not-too-fun illnesses it may carry. Check often for ticks, especially on your head, armpits, and groin. Also look under clothes in areas like the waistband of your pants.

The best removal method is to grasp the tick near the head and pull straight back. You can use a fancy tick-removal tool if you have one; otherwise, tweezers are your best bet. Avoid squeezing the body of the tick; that might push tick juice into the wound. Coaxing a tick to back out with a hot needle, match, or petroleum jelly is an old wives' tale. Ticks close their mouths once they've latched on to a host, and unless you pull them off, they only let go when they're done feeding.

80 GET RID OF A LEECH

Leeches are sneaky, waterborne, bloodsucking worms that attach themselves to your skin with suckers (which, conveniently, they have at both ends). The best defense is to cover your body and tuck your pants into your boots. To dislodge a leech, slide your fingernail under a sucker. Work fast, since the leech will try to reattach itself while you're working on the sucker at the opposite end. Clean the wound to prevent infection.

81
KEEP MOSQUITOES AT BAY

Mosquitoes are attracted to dark clothing, perspiration, carbon dioxide from your breath, lactic acid produced by exercise, and sweet smells like perfume and deodorant. So don't wear dark clothes, and when you exercise, don't get sweaty or breathe heavily. And don't wear aftershave.

Those things are easier said than done (except for shunning aftershave), but there are lots of ways to avoid mosquito bites. Natural repellents include oils made from cinnamon, cedar, eucalyptus, and several types of flowers. In the wild, where those oils might be unavailable, coat your skin with mud and sit near a smoky fire. Making camp on a windy ridgeline also helps keep mosquitoes away.

82
BANISH A BOTFLY

The botfly is native to Central and South America, and it likes to procreate by depositing its eggs on the flesh of human hosts (yes, you). And those eggs grow into larvae that burrow inside (yes, inside you). Worst of all, the larvae have spines that create pain.

To coax out an invader, tie raw bacon over the area for three days; when you take it off, you'll see that the offender has burrowed out of your arm into the meat.

If you'd rather see it dead, suffocate it by putting tree sap, nail polish, or petroleum jelly over the wound, then squeeze out its corpse the next day.

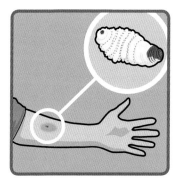

83 SCOUT FOR SHELTER

The fundamental purpose of shelter is to protect your body from the elements. When you're hunting for a prime shelter spot, look for one that does three things: keeps you dry, fends off the wind, and provides shade. Here are some location-scouting tips.

THINK ABOUT TOPOGRAPHY A rock overhang or cave can provide good protection. And you might want to avoid ridges (which tend to be windy) and low-lying land near water (where cold air hovers).

LOOK FOR THE MIDDLE Another good option is a level spot with good drainage on the middle one-third of a hill. These spots tend to have the most comfortable temperature and, if you're lucky, also block the wind.

CONSIDER CRITTERS Avoid dense brush where bugs live and opt for sites that are off the ground or behind rock formations—they'll protect you from predators.

84 CUT SAPLINGS FOR SHELTER

If you find yourself in need of a shelter, you can gather the wood to construct one by felling a tree. If you can bend a green sapling, you can cut it with a sharp knife, but it helps if you bend the trunk back and forth several times to weaken the wood fibers before bringing your knife to bear on it. To cut a sapling, hold it bent with one hand and then press down on the outside of the curve with your knife blade angled slightly. Rock the blade as you cut while maintaining steady downward pressure. Support the tree trunk as you work to keep it from splintering, which would make it difficult for you to finish cutting it.

85 BUILD A DEBRIS HUT

Survival experts agree on this: Your chances of making it through a rough situation increase if you've practiced the skills needed to soldier through an emergency. Here's how to build a debris hut.

First, choose a partner with a mind-set similar to yours. Not only will a buddy provide moral support, but you can monitor each other's physical conditions to make sure no one gets in trouble. Choose a clear night with lows in the upper 20s° to 30s°F (-7° to -1°C)—cool enough to make the drill real, but nothing close to life-threatening. And choose a location where you can pull the plug and drive home if you need to. Or spend an hour in a warm vehicle, at least.

FIND a ridge pole twice as long as your height.

PROP UP one end of the ridge pole on a stump or fallen log about waist high. In a pinch, use two shorter poles with a Y at one end to hold the ridge pole in place. Check the dimensions by lying down under the ridge pole with your feet at the low end. You want 1 to 2 feet (30.5 to 61 cm) of space between your toes and the pole to provide enough room for insulation.

PLACE wrist-thick branches perpendicular to the ridge poles to form A-shaped sidewalls. Then add a layer of smaller branches and fine brush parallel to the ridge poles; these structures will help hold the insulation in place.

COVER the entire framework with dry leaves, grasses, and other debris. You'll need walls at least 2 feet thick. Then place more upright branches and sticks on top of the debris layer to anchor the insulation in place.

STUFF the shelter with more debris and be sure to pile up enough at the entrance that you'll be able to plug the door once you crawl in.

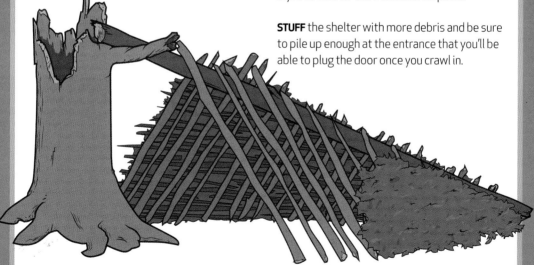

86 UPGRADE THE SHELTER

Ducking into a temporary shelter to quickly get out of the elements is one thing, but if you need to live in that ramshackle space for a prolonged period of time, you'll want to make some home improvements.

CALL IN REINFORCEMENTS Use boulders or the upturned root system of downed trees for a basic framework. Gather heavy branches and layer them onto your exterior walls for further protection. If you have a rain poncho or tarp, spread it over the boughs to keep rainwater from pooling inside.

LAY A FOUNDATION Scrape together a deep layer of pine needles or leaves, then add tender boughs to create a soft, insulated floor that's about 8 inches (20 cm) thick. Position logs or stones around the perimeter to hold the floor materials in place. Do the same to a cave floor.

LOOK UP For long stays, you need food storage. You don't want to sleep with that deer carcass, so hang it away from your shelter and out of predators' reach.

LOOK DOWN May as well make yourself at home with a go-to bathroom spot. Go lower in elevation and a healthy distance downwind to dig your latrine, and, if you're sheltering near your water source, make sure to dig at least 100 feet (30 m) away from it so you don't contaminate your own drinking water.

87

BED DOWN ON A CLIFF

You're stuck on the face of a cliff. In the fading daylight, you realize you're going to have to spend the night. How will you sleep without falling to your death?

Here's a tip from mountaineers: String up a lightweight fabric hammock (if you have one on hand), anchoring each end to the rock wall with pitons or crevice anchors. Then gingerly position yourself in this hammock and try to enjoy a good night's rest with nothing but a sheer drop beneath you. For safety, remain tied to well-anchored ropes, just in case you roll over in your sleep. If you make a mistake here, you give a whole new meaning to falling out of bed. Sweet dreams!

88 MAKE A BED IN A PINCH

Too posh to sleep in a garbage bag? Not if you want to stay dry. A large plastic trash bag can serve as a waterproof body covering. For insulation, stuff the bag with leaves, pine needles, and dry grasses.

 # BUILD A SWAMP SHELTER

You're in the swamp. The ground is wet. The air is wet. And the vegetation is bloated with water, which makes it a poor building material. As a result, one of the most challenging things to do is erect a dry shelter.

STEP 1 Find a dry spot. Of course, "dry" is relative, but a slight hill should be less wet than areas of lower elevation. It's also a good idea to learn how to spot and avoid run-offs. These sparsely vegetated, eroded spots are prone to flash floods, so they're not ideal for a shelter, especially when rainfall is likely.

STEP 2 Look for a space that's at least a little longer than your body and twice as wide, ideally with four trees at the corners. If you can't find a place with well-spaced trees, try driving sturdy wooden stakes into the ground. (Bamboo works nicely.) A rare benefit of building a shelter in a swamp is that it's relatively easy to plunge stakes into the soggy ground.

STEP 3 Measure and cut branches to build a frame. You'll need two rails that are longer than your body and long enough to connect to your trees or poles. Use a square lashing to secure each rail to the trees or posts. If you don't have rope, gather vines, which you can usually find in most swamp and jungle areas.

STEP 4 Once the frame is in place, cut shorter branches to lay across the frame as a platform and tie them to the rails. When you're done, your swamp shelter should be strong enough to hold your full weight and keep you off the ground and at least somewhat drier.

STEP 5 For padding and insulation, top off the platform with large leaves or cut sections of moss. And there you've got it: a fairly comfortable bed that's high above the moisture, not to mention beyond the reach of many animals and insects.

90 TIE A SQUARE LASHING

When you need to build a temporary structure in a hurry, go with square lashing: It's a quick and effective way to secure two posts together.

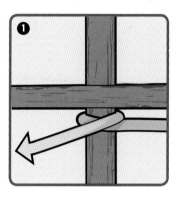

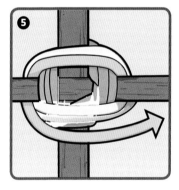

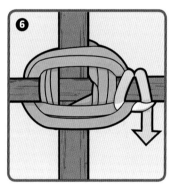

STEP 1 Cross the poles. Wrap rope around the bottom post, with the active end—the end you'll be looping around the poles—on top. Leave a fair amount of rope on the active end.

STEP 2 Wrap the active end around the post, threading it under the first wrap. (This is called a clove hitch, and it's the basis of your knot.)

STEP 3 Twist the static end around the rope's active end. Then weave the active end around the posts, wrapping so the rope goes behind the vertical post, over the horizontal post, and under the vertical post again.

STEP 4 Repeat this wrap two more times, pulling on the rope to tighten as you go.

STEP 5 Wrap the rope so it crosses in front of the vertical post and behind the horizontal one. Repeat several times.

STEP 6 When the knot is sturdy enough, tie it off with a clove hitch, wrapping the active end around the horizontal pole to make a loop, looping around the pole again and threading it through the first loop.

91 HEAL WITH BUGS

Typically, you want to avoid bugs as much as possible. That is, of course, unless they can be of use to you.

WEB BANDAGES A spiderweb can make a sterile bandage for a small cut or abrasion. Find a web and smear it over the injury to prevent infection.

TISSUE THERAPY Maggots are great for removing decayed flesh. Place the insects in a wound and let them feast until only healthy pink tissue remains.

ANT SUTURES Use ants to close a wound. Let them bite both sides of a laceration, then break off their bodies, leaving their heads and mandibles attached.

92 BEAT BLISTERS WITH DUCT TAPE

STEP 1 Drain the blister with a sterilized needle or knife tip. Insert the tip into the base of the blister, then press out the fluid. Keep the flap of skin intact.

STEP 2 Cut a hole slightly larger than the blister in some pliable cloth. Put a second layer on top and seal this "doughnut bandage" to your foot with duct tape.

93 HARVEST ASPIRIN FROM TREE BARK

You've got a sprained ankle, and you've run out of aspirin or, worse, forgot to include aspirin in your kit. Good thing certain trees contain salicin, a relative of aspirin, and it's pretty simple to use them to improvise your own painkiller.

STEP 1 Find yourself a willow or poplar tree if at all possible.

STEP 2 The salicin is located in the tree's soft inner bark, between the hard exterior bark and the hardwood. In younger trees, simply pull off the green bark. If you're dealing with an older tree, use a knife to skin the harder stuff. Scrape the interior of the bark until you have a handful of pulp.

STEP 3 If you're in a hurry, chew the bark at once. If you have the time, boil a handful of pulp in water for 10 minutes. Drink a few glasses a day of this tea, and you'll be back on your feet in no time.

Willow Tree   Poplar Tree

94

HUNT FOR WATER

No matter where you might find yourself, water is a top priority. Finding it, however, can be tricky. Here are some ideas to help you locate this necessary element of survival.

DIG A SEEP HOLE In damp ground, water oozes into a depression. So make a small hole and, over time, enough water will accumulate for you to drink. To collect the water for purification, dip your canteen (or another small container) into the puddle.

FOLLOW THE ANIMALS Bees and flies need water, as do birds. And frogs are a sure indicator that water is near, so trust your eyes and ears and follow the herd.

FIND "WATER POCKETS" Depressions on the tops of boulders or mesas capture and hold rainwater. Use a cloth to soak up the water if there's only a little bit, then be sure to purify it before drinking.

MAKE A STRAW Use a hollow reed to draw water from inaccessible places, then release it into a container so you can purify it. Also, don't consider the reed a "one-time use" tool. Carry it with you in case you come across water later.

DESALINATE SEAWATER Boil water in a container and capture the steam with a cloth. When the fabric is saturated, wring the water out into a clean container.

95 GET WATER FROM A BAG

One of the quickest, easiest, and most effective ways of gathering emergency water in a vegetated environment is to mine the leaves of surrounding trees and bushes. It's a snap, and it can save your life.

Look for a leafy tree in bright sunshine. Place a small rock in a plastic bag, then shimmy the bag over a leafy limb. Be careful not to puncture the bag. Blow the bag up to create smooth surfaces for water condensation. Tie off the bag opening as tightly as possible. Work the rock down into the end of the bag so that one corner of the bag is lower than the ends of the limbs. As sunlight heats the bag and vegetation, evaporated water will condense on the bag's inner surface and drip into the lowest corner. Simply pour it out or insert a length of tubing or a hollow grass reed into the mouth of the bag so you can drain the collected water without removing the bag from the limb. Don't forget to purify water collected in the wild.

96

KNOW YOUR WATER

Safe drinking water can make or break an emergency situation. It's never wise to drink raw water from sources in the wild. Pathogens and contaminants can taint the water supply and cause serious harm or death if consumed without the right treatment. Consider these methods to deal with problems.

	EFFECT	METHOD
BACTERIA AND VIRUSES	These can cause diarrhea, vomiting, dysentery, and death.	Boiling, chemical disinfection, UV devices, and water filters
PROTOZOA	These can cause diarrhea, dysentery, and death.	Boiling, chemical disinfection, and water filters
PARASITES	Fluke worms and other parasites can cause liver damage, lung ailments, and a host of odd symptoms that are potentially fatal.	Boiling, chemical disinfection, and water filters

97 PURIFY WATER IN THE WILD

That fresh mountain stream you see in beer commercials? It's actually chock-full of nasties that can kill you if you're not careful.

There are three steps to making water ready to drink: filtering, boiling, and treating it chemically. Start by filtering it (a coffee filter or a cloth makes a good sieve) to remove artificial contaminants and sediment. Then purify it by boiling and chemically treating it.

Bringing water to a boil kills organic critters (such as viruses and bugs); treating with iodine or water-purification tablets removes everything else. Most survival kits include these agents.

When faced with the prospect of drinking contaminated water, weigh the risks of illness against the risks of death from dehydration. You don't want to get sick, but choosing to drink might save your life.

98 FILTER WATER WITH YOUR PANTS

Yes, you can use a bag if you have one, but a cut-off pant leg makes a great water filter. Modesty must give way to survival, so don't be shy about making the most of your denim: Rescuers won't care if they find you wandering around in short shorts. To turn a pant leg into a filter, tie off the bottom and add alternating layers of gravel and sand to trap particles of debris. Slowly add water to the top of the filter, allowing it to trickle down through the layers into a catch basin. The water in this basin is ready for the next step in the purification process—boiling.

DO allow cloudy water to settle before filtering or chemically treating it. If water is cold, wait at least 30 minutes after chemical treatment before drinking.

DON'T drink from a stagnant pool of water where there are dead animals around—their decaying bodies may have poisoned the water. Safe water should also support plant life, so look for greenery. Don't consider "wild" water to be safe for consumption until you've treated it.

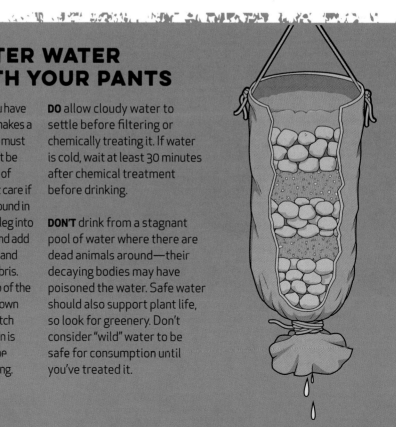

99

LET THE SUN SHINE IN

If you have a clear glass or plastic bottle, some water, and a sunny day, you can use the sun's light to make your water much safer to drink. Largely advocated for developing countries, solar water disinfection is gaining some traction in the survival-skills crowd; and it's a great fit for equatorial countries with abundant strong sunlight but few other resources.

The most common solar disinfection technique is to expose clear plastic bottles full of questionable water to the sun for a minimum of one day. The sun's UV light kills or damages almost all biological hazards in the water. This method has many advantages: It's easy to use; it's free; and it offers good (but not complete) bacterial and viral disinfection.

There are some problems with this method, though. You need sunny weather (or two days of overcast sky) to reach the maximum effectiveness. You cannot use it in rainy weather. It offers no residual disinfection. It may be less effective against bacterial spores and cyst stages of some parasites. Both the water and the bottle need to be very clear. And finally, it only works with bottles that are 2 liters or smaller in volume.

While solar disinfection isn't 100 percent effective, it's still a lot better than taking your chances by drinking raw water.

BUILD A ONE-MATCH FIRE WHEN YOUR LIFE DEPENDS ON IT

If things are so bad that you're down to one match, then it's no time for you to be taking chances. The secret to last-chance fire building is attention to detail long before the match comes out of your pocket.

STEP 1 Begin with tinder. Collect three times as much as you think you'll need; don't stop looking until you have a double handful. Shred it well; what you're going for is a fiberlike consistency.

Conifer pitch, pine needles, cedar bark, birch bark, and dry bulrushes all make excellent natural tinder. Lots of other common items make good fire-starting material, too. Turn your pockets inside out to look for lint or candy bar wrappers. Duct tape burns like crazy; maybe there's a strip stuck to your gun case. Wader patch glue and plastic arrow fletching will work, too. The more variety you have, the longer the burn.

STEP 2 Gather twice as much kindling as you think you're going to need and separate it into piles of like-size pieces. If you have to stop what you're doing and fumble for a pencil-size piece of pine at the wrong moment, your fire will go up in smoke. Your piles should consist of pieces the diameter of a red wiggler, of a .22 cartridge, and of a 20-gauge shell. Use a knife to fuzz up the outer edges of a few sticks for a quicker catch.

STEP 3 Start small. Use two-thirds of your tinder to begin with and save the other third in case you need a second try with the dying embers of your first shot. Arrangement is important: You want to be able to get your match head near the bottom of the pile, and you also want to ensure that the slightest breeze pushes emerging flames toward your materials. Blow gently on the flames and feed only the fast-burning ones.

101 BUILD SURVIVAL SKILLS

Everything that's in these pages can be considered a survival skill, but some situations are a little bit more immediate than others. After all, if you need to learn to garden, there's probably time for someone to teach you. If you need to learn how to win in a fistfight, that's a good thing to know before the brawl breaks out. The skills below will help keep you alive and unharmed when the chips are down.

READ A MAP Don't just rely on a GPS or smartphone's navigation software. Know your way around a real map, on paper. Learn how to find where you are and how to get where you're going—and you should know how a compass works, too.

BUILD A FIRE This is one of humanity's oldest and most important skills. Even if you have matches or a lighter with you, you should learn how to start a fire without them; it's a skill that might save your life.

SWIM You'd be surprised how many people don't know how to swim (or aren't confident in their abilities), and considering that more than 70 percent of the Earth's surface is covered by water, it's a lifesaving skill. If all else fails, you should at least know how to tread water and how to float on your back.

RIDE A HORSE You don't have to make like the Lone Ranger, but in a hard-core survival situation, horses might be your best or only form of transport. Knowing how to saddle up and ride with some skill will keep you from being sore, laughed at, or left behind. Extra points for mastering the art of mounting and riding bareback.

KNOW BASIC FIRST AID Even knowing how to take care of minor injuries can make a big difference in a difficult situation. Add in some CPR training and the Heimlich maneuver, and you're well on your way to the foundations of medical care.

TAKE AND THROW A PUNCH You might hope never to get into a fight, but if push comes to shove (or jab, or hook, or uppercut), you should learn how to defend yourself and others with your bare hands.

HANDLE A GUN Plenty of people are unreasonably afraid of guns simply because they don't know very much about them. Even if you've never hunted or don't expect to have to defend yourself, take a basic firearms course at a local shooting range. You'll learn how to safely handle and use a gun, should the need ever arise.

102 TEST PLANTS FOR EDIBILITY

The key to ensuring that a plant is safe to eat is executing each step with plenty of time in between; if you wait 30 minutes and monitor yourself for a bad reaction, you'll learn what you can stomach and what you can cast aside.

STEP 1 Divide all the plants into separate parts and test each one. If one part is toxic, you can weed it out without discarding other parts.

STEP 2 Smell each part; if it's stinky, don't eat it.

STEP 3 Rub the plant part on your lips and monitor your reaction.

STEP 4 If you didn't get bad vibes from the lip contact, touch the plant to your tongue.

STEP 5 If all's still well, graduate to chewing and holding the plant in your mouth.

STEP 6 Try swallowing a small amount. If your stomach doesn't reject it, then feast away.

Boiled or Cooked Nettle Leaves and Stems

Raw, Cooked, or Dried Seaweed Leaves

Cooked Cattail Leaf Shoots and Summer Flower Heads

Boiled or Baked Young Pine Cones and Raw Pine Cone Seeds

103 SURVIVE ON ACORNS

Stick with acorns from the white oak family (white oak, chestnut oak, bur oak), which have less tannin than red oak nuts. Cull any nuts with a tiny hole in the husk—this is made by an acorn weevil. Remove the cap and shell the rest with a knife or pliers from a multitool.

THE EASY WAY TO EAT ACORNS
To leach out the tannins, tie the nuts in a T-shirt. Submerge it in a running stream for several hours. Taste occasionally to test for bitterness. Or boil the nuts, changing the water frequently until it runs fairly clear. Then roast near a fire. Eat as is or grind into flour.

THE HARD WAY TO EAT ACORNS
Grind or pound shelled acorns, then mix with enough water to create a paste. Place a clean cloth in a wire sieve, scoop the acorn mush on top, and run fresh cold water over the mixture, squeezing water through the mush and out through the sieve. Taste occasionally, until the bitterness is removed. Use as a coarse meal like grits or pound it into finer flour.

104 STEER CLEAR OF POISONOUS PLANTS

It's no fun getting poked and stung while beating your way through the bush. To protect your skin against thorns and stinging nettles, wear long pants and long sleeves and don leather gloves that'll let you move plants aside with ease. Use a long stick to open up a path through a thicket and employ your well-shod feet to mash plants down out of your way. But if you can identify a plant as poisonous, don't walk through it; the itch-inducing resin collects on your clothing and boots and might eventually get transferred to your skin.

Poison Oak

Poison Sumac

Poison Ivy

105

IMPROVISE A SKEWER HOOK

If you don't have a regular skewer hook, you can make one from a needle-shape sliver of sharpened hardwood or bone. Tie a line to the middle of the skewer and put a daub of tree sap on the knot to keep it from slipping off. Then turn the skewer parallel with the fishing line and bury it in the bait. When the fish takes the bait, the skewer turns sideways, hooking the fish. And there you have it—fresh fish for supper, no matter where you happen to be!

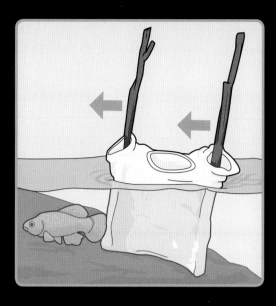

106

FISH WITH YOUR SHIRT

Fishing is a great way to supplement your survival diet. If you don't have a rod and reel handy, you can use this makeshift net to catch small fish. Insert two poles through the sleeves of a basic T-shirt and out through the shirt's bottom. Tie off the excess fabric with simple overhand knots if desired, but spreading the poles apart should be enough to keep the "net" in place. Now simply herd fish into the shallows or scoop them up with the net.

107

SPEAR FISH IN A FUNNEL TRAP

Make the walls of the funnel trap with piled-up stones or tightly spaced sticks driven solidly into the river or lakebed. Once fish are in the trap, close the entrance, roil the water, and either spear them or net them with a seine made by tying a shirt or other cloth between two stout poles.

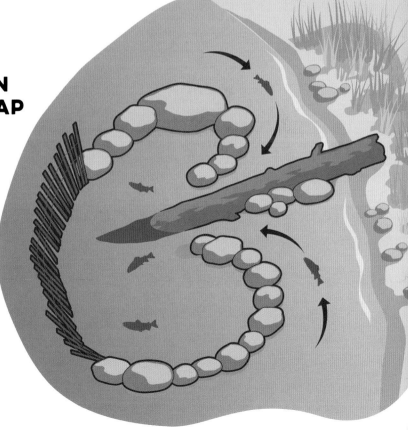

108 BAIT YOUR TRAP CORRECTLY

When it comes to trapping, you need to use the right bait. Herbivores and carnivores will obviously go for different things—and even omnivores can be tricky.

BAIT FOR HERBIVORES There are plenty of vegetarian baits to choose from. Groundhogs go for sweet apples cut into pieces so their fragrance is released. Squirrels are very fond of whole peanuts, and they have a hard time resisting crushed sweet pecans and hickories. Just don't try using them under a tree full of those nuts. The animals won't go for the human-tainted bait when there is plenty of the same food lying nearby.

BAIT FOR OMNIVORES Omnivores, by definition, will eat anything. This can make them either easier or harder to bait. For raccoons, you can use canned tuna or sardines. The fouler and cheaper the fish, the better. You can often trap for raccoons alongside creeks and streams, pouring the tuna juice from the cans into the creek so they'll follow the creek to get their fishy treat. Possums love lunchmeat, hot dogs, and other processed-meat foods.

BAIT FOR CARNIVORES Meat eaters do have their preferences. Coyotes love beaver meat. Foxes love rotten hard-boiled eggs. Mink, ermine, and fisher cats love fish. Bobcats love fresh organ meat like liver and lung. You can also use various scent baits—it doesn't have to be food. Coyote and beaver scent can be used for coyotes. And coon urine can be a useful cover scent against other animals as well as for attracting raccoons.

109 COVER YOUR SCENT

Though trappers use many different types of traps, they all have the same problem: They've got human scent all over them. To have any luck when dealing with wild animals, you need to fool their noses. Follow these tips to de-scent your traps and hands with nature itself.

USE MUD Start by washing your hands and any questionable trap parts in the local waterway. Use available sand, clay, mud, or silt as an abrasive and oil absorber.

POWDER WITH BLACK CHARCOAL As your hands and trap parts are drying, you can wipe them with powdered black charcoal from the campfire. Don't use the white or gray ashes; just grind black charcoal chunks into a powder and apply it.

LAYER WITH PLANTS Use a strong-smelling local plant as another cover scent. Crushed pine needles, wild onions, mints, and other pungent plants can hide your stink. Just stay out of the poison oak.

GET DIRTY The final touch in this layering system is fresh, damp, local dirt. Rub it generously on your hands and the trap parts as a final cover and scent absorber.

110 BUILD A DEADFALL

One of the best traps is the Paiute deadfall, dating back to the early Paiute Indians. Like all deadfalls, there is some type of weight and a trigger system to hold up part of the rock until your future meal gets under there. What makes this deadfall different is the stronger, more sensitive trigger that can be fashioned without a knife. Just break a few sticks into the right sizes, scrounge up a bit of string, and grab a flat rock.

STEP 1 Gather the sticks and other supplies. For an average-size rodent, you'll need the following: a Y-shaped stick thicker than a pencil and about 8 inches (20 cm) long; a straight stick thicker than a pencil, about 9 inches (23 cm) long; a 2-inch (5-cm) stick that is a little skinnier than a pencil; a slender bait stick half the diameter of a pencil and about 12 inches (30 cm) long; about 8 inches (20 cm) of string; appropriate bait for your critter of choice; and a flat rock that weighs 5–10 pounds (2–5 kg).

STEP 2 Take your 9-inch (23-cm) straight stick (this is called the lever) and tie one end of the string to it. Tie the other end to the 2-inch (5-cm) stick (the toggle). Square knots are fine. Wipe or skewer the bait on one end of the 12-inch (30-cm) bait stick.

STEP 3 Set the trap by laying the rock down on a hard patch of ground. Stand up the Y-shaped stick (the post) by the edge of the rock. Put the stringless end of the lever in the fork of the post, with a small portion of it sticking out toward the rock. Place the rock on the tip of the lever. You should be able to hold the weight of the rock by only holding down the string end of the lever. Now wrap the toggle halfway around the post. Place the baited end of the bait stick between a rough spot under the stone and the tip of the toggle. When you can let go of the trigger stick and the rock stays up, you know you did it right.

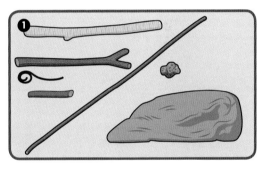

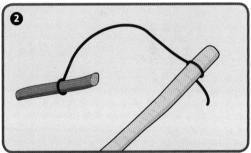

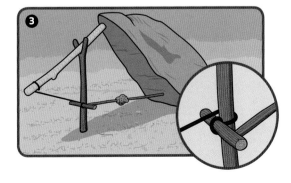

111 GOBBLE UP BUGS

Don't be deceived by their less-than-delicious appearance: Some bugs are edible, while others contain toxins. These are your safest bets:

GRUBS Beetle larvae are fine to eat plain and live or, if you want to be fancy, as an addition to soup.

GRASSHOPPERS Skewer grasshoppers on a thin stick and roast them over the coals of your campfire.

ANTS These trail snacks taste like lemon drops, thanks to the formic acid in their systems. Just

pop them in your mouth and chew—unless it's a fire ant, a bullet ant, or another ant that bites. Avoid those!

SCORPIONS Pin the critter down with a knife, cut off its claws and stinger, and roast or toss in soup.

BEETLES Some are edible; some will make you sick. Don't eat them unless you gain local knowledge first.

112

DIG A HOLE TRAP

Another way to catch an animal is to dig a hole 3 feet (1 m) deep with an opening as big as your fist and walls that get wider toward the bottom, like a soft triangle shape. Lay a small log, elevated slightly by stones or other debris, over the top of the hole. With any luck, a critter will scurry under the log for cover and fall into the hole, and the hole's sloped walls will prevent it from climbing out. Dinner will fall in your lap. And remember, in this situation, beggars can't be choosers.

113 EAT ROADKILL

If you make it to a road, rescue is likely just around the corner. If not, however, even the least-traveled highways can serve as a buffet for the feral forager. To separate plateworthy roadkill from vulture food, follow these guidelines:

BODY CHECK Look for critters that have been clipped and tossed to the side of the road. If you have to use a flat shovel to retrieve your prize, well...

SMELL TEST Any hunter knows what fresh dead meat smells like. Give the carcass a good sniff. If it smells fresh, it's good to go.

CLOUDY EYES Pass it up; it's been dead awhile.

FLEA CHECK If you find maggots, keep it out of your shopping cart. Fleas and ticks, however, are a good indicator of a fresh kill.

114 CALL FOR HELP IN ANY LANGUAGE

The international signal for distress is a sequence of short and long signals, designed for telegraph operators—three short, three long, three short. Adopted at the Berlin Radiotelegraphic Conference in 1906, the SOS sequence was based solely on its ease of transmitting. It does not mean "save our ship" or anything else you've heard. But you can transmit the code with just about any device imaginable: whistle blasts, car horns, gunshots, light flashes, even pots and pans.

115 WHITTLE A WHISTLE OUT OF A STICK

Cut and peel the bark from a finger-length section of any stick with a soft pith, such as elder. Next, use a thin twig to bore out this pith, leaving a hollow cylinder (a). With a knife cut a notch near one end (b). Whittle a smaller piece of wood that will fit snugly into the notch end and then slice a little off the top of that plug to allow for the passage of air (c). Fit the plug into the cylinder, trimming the end to shape (d). Place your finger in the other end and blow into the mouthpiece to force the air over the notch in the top of the whistle. When you get a clear whistle, the plug is well fitted. Permanently plug the end of the cylinder with a short piece of wood (e).

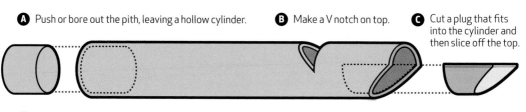

A Push or bore out the pith, leaving a hollow cylinder.

B Make a V notch on top.

C Cut a plug that fits into the cylinder and then slice off the top.

E Completely plug this end.

D Fit the plug into the cylinder.

116 AIM A MAKESHIFT SIGNAL MIRROR

The best commercial signal mirrors are made with aiming devices. But there are ways to aim a jerry-rigged signal mirror—aluminum foil wrapped neatly around a playing card or the shiny interior surface of an aluminum can—that can also attract attention.

FOR A MOVING TARGET

STEP 1 Hold the mirror in one hand and extend the other in front, fingers spread to form a V between your fingers and thumb.

STEP 2 Move your hand until the target rests in the V.

STEP 3 Angle the mirror so the reflected sunlight flashes through the V and directly onto the target.

FOR A STATIONARY TARGET

STEP 1 Drive an aiming stake chest-high into the ground or choose a similar object such as a broken sapling or rock.

STEP 2 Stand so the target, the top of the aiming stake, and the signal mirror are in a straight line.

STEP 3 Move the mirror so the reflected sunlight flashes from the top of the aiming stake to the target.

117 GET NOTICED BY RESCUERS

Let's face it: The great outdoors isn't all that great when you're stuck in the wilderness and need assistance—and quick. Ideally, you already have key rescue tools (such as fire-starting equipment and both audible and visible signal devices) at your disposal. If all else fails, use these tactics to hasten your rescue.

SCOUT WISELY Make yourself more visible by positioning yourself in a clearing or at a higher elevation. This placement allows you to be both seen and heard from a greater distance.

SHINE A LIGHT Use a signal mirror during daylight hours. If you don't have a mirror handy, check your possessions for any metal object that you can work into a shine.

EMPLOY YOUR GADGETS Try your cell phone or two-way radio and turn on your personal locator beacon (PLB). Don't leave your phone on to search for a signal; the battery will drain quickly. Instead, turn it on at intervals as you travel and cross your fingers.

SIGNAL WITH FIRE Set up three signal fires (widely recognized as a distress signal) and keep an ignition source handy. At any sign that a rescuer might be nearby, get all the fires going. The smoke will attract attention by day, and the flames will draw it by night.

SPELL IT OUT Use color, contrast, and an SOS symbol on the ground to attract the eyes of searchers.

MAKE A MESS Disturb your surroundings to signal that things aren't right by beating down tall grasses, knocking over saplings, removing tree branches, and pushing rocks around.

SEND UP A FLAG Hoist a colored fabric panel to serve as a wind-driven signal flag.

118 LIGHT UP A SIGNAL FIRE

You can use fire as an effective cry for help. Build a signal fire in a location that's open and elevated so that both the smoke and the light are visible.

THINK ABOUT CONTRAST Almost all natural fire fuel (vegetation) produces white smoke. If the weather's cloudy or foggy, no one will notice your white signal. Throw a few ounces of cooking oil, brake fluid, or any other oily substance into the fire to produce black smoke, which is much more noticeable.

PREVENT RUNAWAY FIRES The middle of dry grasslands on a breezy day is a very bad place to start a big fire. And never let a fire get so big that you can't put it out with what you have on hand.

119 PREVENT A FOREST FIRE

Smokey Bear doesn't like it when your campfire gets away from you—especially if it torches the forest.

START FROM SCRATCH If you have to build a fresh fire base, look for a site that's at least 16 feet from bushes, dry grasses, and other flammable objects. Avoid overhead foliage, too. Clear a spot 9 feet in diameter, removing twigs, leaves, and anything else that can burn. Dig a pit in the soil 12 inches deep. Circle the pit with rocks. When you're done with the fire, pour water on it or use dirt to smother the embers.

PICK A SPOT THAT HAS BURNED BEFORE The safest spot to build a fire is an existing fire pit because surrounding flammable materials have already burned.

EXTREME CONDITIONS

GO TO EXTREMES—AND GET OUT.

Polar explorer Ernest Shackleton (1874-1922) was famous for many things, not the least of which was his endurance. "Difficulties," he said, "are just things to overcome, after all." Survival in any wild place takes nerve and know-how, but in extreme enviornments such as the Arctic or the desert, it takes these in spades. Much of the value of knowing how to stay alive when you lose all your chips is that knowledge will help you play a better hand when you're still holding a few decent cards. If you ever have to cross a raging river, escape a wildfire, get yourself out of the bottom of a canyon, or punch a polar bear in the nose, you will be very glad you brushed up on these tips for survival in the world's most severe places.

120

SURVIVE A WILDFIRE

During a wildfire, the most dangerous places to be are uphill or downwind from the flames. If the wind is blowing toward the fire, run into the wind. But if it's behind the fire, you need to move away even faster—that fire will be coming on quick.

If you're caught out in the open, move to an area that has already burned over—not to an area that is in danger of being burned. Avoid canyons and other natural chimneys. Get into a river or lake, if possible. Look for breaks in the trees, which could mean breaks in the firestorm. If you're near a road, lie facedown along the road or in a ditch or depression on the uphill side. Cover up with anything that provides a shield against the heat.

121 CROSS A SWOLLEN CREEK OR (SLIGHTLY) RAGING RIVER

Look before you leap. Current moves most swiftly where a stream narrows, so try crossing at a wider, shallower spot. Scout the far shore to make sure you can clamber to safety—no slick mudbanks or bluffs. Unhook hip belts and loosen shoulder straps on packs in case you need to jettison your load before going into the drink. Cut a shoulder-high staff or break out the trekking poles and remove your socks and insoles. Wet shoes are easier to tolerate than wet everything. Lace your boots firmly and then cross the stream diagonally, moving sideways like a crab and slightly downstream, yielding to the current. Nice and easy keeps you upright. Move only one point of contact at a time: Plant your staff, take a step, plant your staff, take another.

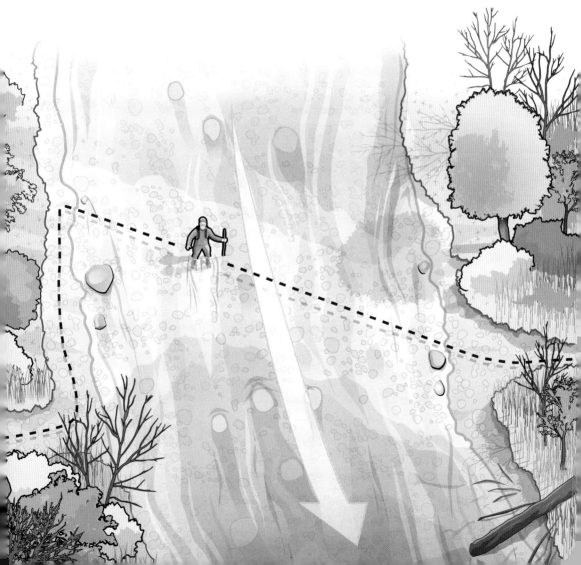

122 FORD A RIVER WITH FRIENDS

Sometimes you might not be able to wait around for someone to build a safe water crossing. Fording swift-moving water can be dangerous, but if you apply some basic triangular geometry, it can help you cross safely. If you are braving the current and you are backed up by two friends on shore—with a sturdy loop of rope twice the width of the body of water connecting all three of you—the two on land will be able to help you, even if you lose your footing. Once you reach the far bank, the second can cross, using the rope stretched between the banks as a safety line. When the last person is ready to cross, he or she can enter the water and be pulled across by the two on the far shore holding the rope.

Other tips for safety: Face upstream while you cross, leave your shoes on to protect your feet and give you better grip, shuffle your feet along the bottom, and avoid lifting your feet. If the conditions are not favorable at one site, look for a better spot to cross.

123 AVOID A LIGHTNING STRIKE

If you can see it, flee it! But what do you do when you're caught outdoors with almost nowhere to hide? Try this.

OUT CAMPING Avoid open fields and ridgetops. Stay away from tall isolated trees, fence lines, and metal. A tent provides no protection.

IN OPEN COUNTRY Avoid high ground and points of contact with dissimilar objects, such as water and land, boulders and land, or single trees and land. Head for ditches, gullies, or low ground. Spread out: Group members should be at least 15 feet apart (4.6 m).

ON THE WATER Head inside a boat cabin, which offers a safer environment. Stay off the radio unless it is an emergency. Drop anchor and get as low in the boat as possible. If you're in a canoe on open water, get as low in the canoe as possible and as far as possible from any metal object. If shore only offers rocky crags and tall isolated trees, stay in the boat.

AT THE LAST MOMENT Many experts believe that the "lightning crunch" provides little to no protection, but at this point, some action is better than nothing. Put your feet together and balance on the balls of your feet. Squat low, tuck your head, close your eyes, and cover your ears.

124 BUILD A BRUSH RAFT

You're thinking: "Build a survival raft? When will I ever need to do that?" Consider this: A hiker in New Mexico's Gila National Forest was trapped on the far side of the Gila River after it rose too high for her to wade back. She managed to survive five weeks before being rescued. In fact, crossing raging rivers is a survival situation outdoorsmen often face.

Here is an easy way to build a brush raft. It's designed to keep your gear dry while you swim and push it ahead of you. Though it's buoyant enough to keep you from drowning, it can't support your full weight. You'll need a poncho (or a tarp), which determines the size of the finished raft. Tie a rope to the raft to hold on to while crossing.

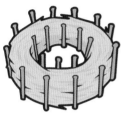

STEP 1 Drive sticks into the ground to outline an inner and outer circle. The diameter should be half the poncho's width. Weave saplings into a doughnut shape, using the stakes as a guide.

STEP 2 Secure the woven materials with whatever cordage is available to you—strong vines, peeled bark from a tree, bootlaces, even strips from your shirt.

STEP 3 Place the brush raft on top of the poncho and put the hood on the inner side of the doughnut. Tie the neck with the drawstring so it won't let in water.

STEP 4 Draw the sides of the poncho up over the raft. Fasten to the brush via grommets or by tying cordage around small stones wrapped in the material.

125

SWIM ACROSS A RAGING RIVER

Even for experienced outdoorsfolk, swimming across deep, moving water is unsettling, but it can be done.

STRIP DOWN Swimming nude is much easier than fighting the weight of waterlogged clothing. Use a trash bag or poncho to keep your things dry—and the

bundle can do double duty as a flotation device.

AIM DOWNSTREAM In rapids, you won't be swimming freestyle across the river. The current is going to pull you downstream fast, so position yourself on your back, with your feet facing downstream. This

position will help protect you against impacts with rocks and submerged snags.

PADDLE Use your hands to paddle and guide yourself toward the far bank. It takes a while to cross rapidly moving water, so swim deliberately and expect to end up downstream

126

SURVIVE IN FAST WATER

Maybe you fell out of your fishing boat, or maybe you slipped while wading the river. Either way, you're suddenly sucked downstream into a long, violent rapid. What do you do?

STEP 1 The safest way to ride a rapid is on your back, with your head pointed upstream, your feet pointing downstream, legs flexed, and toes just above the water's surface. Lift your head to watch ahead. Use your feet to bounce off rocks and logs.

STEP 2 Choking on water can unleash a panic reaction. Avoid a sudden, massive gulp of water by inhaling in the troughs (low points) and exhaling or holding your breath at the crests (tops) of the waves.

STEP 3 You will naturally look downstream to avoid obstacles, such as logjams, but don't forget to also scan the shoreline for calmer water, such as an eddy on the downstream side of a rock or river bend.

STEP 4 As the current carries you toward quieter water, paddle with your arms and kick with your legs to steer yourself toward shore. When you get close, roll onto your stomach and swim upstream at a 45-degree angle, which will ferry you to the bank.

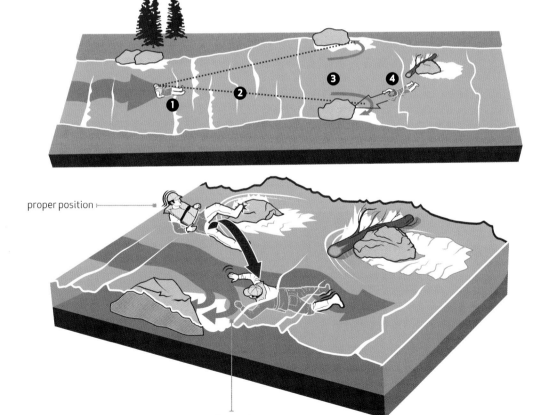

proper position

swim to edge

127 IMPROVISE SNOW GOGGLES

Snow blindness is a real danger that you can easily prevent with a good pair of sunglasses. However, you might not always have a pair handy, especially if weather conditions take you by surprise and you find yourself in a survival situation. So make like the Inuit and fashion your own goggles. First, cut a strip of duct tape 1 foot (30 cm) long and fold it over on itself lengthwise. Then, using a knife or razor blade, cut a single long slit in the folded duct tape. Next, fasten the makeshift goggles around your head with more tape. For added protection, blacken your cheeks with soot or other dark material to help absorb sunlight.

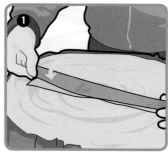

128

MAKE EMERGENCY SNOWSHOES

Whip up these snowshoes, which will help you glide—not plow—across the snow's surface.

STEP ONE Start by cutting two pine boughs with ample foliage to about 3 feet (1 m) long.

STEP TWO Tie a string near the base of the branch, where you cut it. Then flip the branch over and tie an overhand knot on the opposite side.

STEP THREE Place the branch so that its top is face down in the snow, with the foliage bending upward. Step on it, tie the string to your shoe, and thread the line through the shoe-lace eyelets.

STEP FOUR Once you're strapped in, walk normally

across the snow. Your boot will naturally come up from the branch about 30 degrees when you walk, which will keep you from sinking into the snow.

129

NAVIGATE THE ARCTIC

Traveling the taiga or tundra regions of the North is daunting. It is a vast region of Canada with very little infrastructure, meaning you could be out there for weeks or even months without much for resources. You have to deal with dry, extreme temperatures and everything around you will begin to look the same.

SEASONAL CHALLENGES In the winter the Arctic is a barren landscape covered in hard-packed snow. It can be difficult to tell whether you're traveling on ground or ice, and avoiding frost bite or hypothermia is always a challenge. In summer, white snow is replaced with gravel, lichen-covered rocks, and low-growing vegetation. You'll have to navigate the spiderweb of rivers and lakes and at times you'll feel like the black flies could pick you up and carry you away.

WATCH THE SUN AND STARS In summer there can be close to 24 hours of daylight. Use the sun as

your navigational point, knowing it will travel across the sky from east to west over a longer period of time. The sun travels in a big circle, so keeping track of what time of day it is can be key to using the sun for navigation. In the winter it can be dark day and night. When skies are clear enough, the stars can be the only way to navigate.

BUILD AN INUKSUK In the Arctic every hill looks the same and it is easy to walk in circles. The Inuit build inuksuit, the plural of inuksuk, as navigational aids to tell others someone was there or to simply identify the right path. Each stone monument, built in the likeness of man, should be distinct and identifiable so you can use it as a reference point. You'll have to dig deep and remember the days when you played with building blocks. Mark your path with inuksuit by building the figures along the trail and be sure to mark where you've stashed supplies or found abundant food.

130 SPOT HYPOTHERMIA

Hypothermia is a medical condition that occurs when a person's core temperature drops below 95°F (35°C). This dangerous condition can be caused by exposure to water, wind, very cold air, or a combination of these elements. Be alert to these signs in yourself and others in order to catch hypothermia while it is still treatable.

MILD

Shivering • Confusion • Slurred speech • Numbness or tingling in the skin • Sluggish muscles (a good indicator of a cold body before shivering begins)

MODERATE

Violent shivering • Clumsiness • Lack of coordination • Pale skin • Blue-colored lips, ears, fingers, and toes

SEVERE

Difficulty speaking • Trouble walking • Amnesia • Extreme tiredness • Irrational behavior (such as removing clothing or burrowing into snow, sand, or other material)

131 FIGHT BACK AGAINST THE COLD

Rewarming is the main method of treatment for hypothermia victims. Use one of these methods (or a combination of techniques) based on the severity of the cold exposure.

PASSIVE EXTERNAL REWARMING This type of rewarming involves the use of the body's own heat-generating ability. Get the victim out of his wet clothes and into some properly insulated dry clothing and a warm environment. Give a little high-calorie food and warm sips of a hot beverage if the hypothermia is mild.

ACTIVE EXTERNAL REWARMING Apply warming devices externally, such as a hot water bottle in both armpits. Never use hot baths to treat a hypothermic person because it can cause a heart attack.

ACTIVE CORE REWARMING Core rewarming should be administered only by a professional, as it involves the use of intravenous warmed fluids, irrigation of body cavities with warmed fluids, use of warm humidified inhaled air, or use of extracorporeal rewarming such as a heart-lung machine. These techniques are impractical, impossible, or dangerous to attempt in the field. If you are forced to treat this level of hypothermia, be aware that victims often go into shock as they rewarm.

132 FACTOR IN FROSTBITE

Frostbite occurs when ice forms in your skin and tissues. Your skin will often go numb right before frostbite. Later (when the tissues thaw out), there's an intense burning pain. Frostbite can be a common injury during the winter months, especially in northern regions, at high altitude, and under windy conditions. Watch for these signs in yourself and others to prevent frostbite and catch it in the field while it is still treatable.

PREVENT THE PROBLEM The best preventive measure you can take is to recognize the conditions that cause frostbite and to keep all skin warmly covered. Temperatures in the 20° F (-7° C) range can lead to frostbite if strong winds are present or if there has been enough exposure time. Temperatures near or below 0° F (-18° C), with any wind, are swift to produce frostbite on exposed skin and extremities—fingers, toes, ears, and noses. Wind speeds over 20 mph (32 kph) at temperatures below 0°F (-18°C) are very likely to create frostbite in hours or even minutes.

FACE THE FACTS Superficial frostbite commonly occurs in patches on exposed areas of the face, but it can also occur on hands, ears, fingers, and toes. These patches of skin might look dull in color, waxy, and pale and feel firm to the touch. The underlying tissue will still feel soft, and the victim might feel pain in these areas.

DON'T GO TOO FAR Deep frostbite happens when deeper tissues and more extensive tissue become frozen. The skin will be pale and firm, and the underlying tissues will feel solid. Feet, legs, hands, and arms may be lost due to this severe level of frostbite. Tissues with deep frostbite will generally feel numb, and joint movement will feel restricted.

133 LIGHT UP THE DARK

Plain and simple, you should be carrying multiple fire-starting methods on your person during every single outdoor excursion—especially in freezing weather. Without this precious gear, improvising a fire would be a monumental task or, in the worst winter conditions, an impossible one. Fire equals life, and considering its many crucial uses (boiling, heating, lighting, cooking), it makes sense to carry several faithful fire-starters whenever you head to the wild.

134 PUT THE ICE TO WORK

While all due caution should be exercised—always!—when you're out on an icy body of water, it's also important to understand that the ice isn't out to get you. When used in the right way and for the right reasons, ice can become an extremely valuable resource for your survival and the survival of those around you. Here are a few ways to make the treacherous ice work for you.

BUILD WITH ICE A thin slab of ice can be used in a number of ways to help construct a survival snow shelter.

The best uses are as a nice, clear window to let in light (if you have a less cloudy and more manageable section of ice) and as a slab door (for heftier pieces). For each of these projects, select sheets of ice that are clear, free of cracks, and 1 to 2 inches (2.5 to 5 cm) thick. You'll need to be able to move them once they're in place, especially the slab door.

ASSIST YOUR TRAPS Ice slabs make excellent funnels and fencing for trap sites. Use the ice to build walls, holes, paths, gates, and other structures to help direct your prey to just the right spot. Don't worry if your structures are a bit crude—your dinner won't notice.

HEAL WITH COLD Sprains and strains are common injuries when you're in the outdoor wilderness, and relief is close at hand during the winter. Grab a chunk of ice and wrap it in cloth. Use this bundle as a cold pack to reduce swelling and pain in the affected area.

135 BITE BACK

The treatment of frostbite is usually a painful process that involves rewarming the skin and tissues. This can be done in the field or in a hospital, but should only be attempted if there is no danger of refreezing. Here's how to treat frostbite:

STEP 1 Identify the type of frostbite. Superficial frostbite occurs in patches, which may look dull in color and waxy, while deep frostbite causes the skin to turn pale and firm (see item 132).

STEP 2 Rewarm the skin and tissues—unless there is a danger of refreezing. In cases of superficial frostbite, place a warm body part against the frostbitten tissue. Deep frostbite requires hot water at stable temperatures around 105°F (40.5°C). Treat with pain medication as you begin rewarming. Ibuprofen is a good choice for the pain, and it should be taken before the pain becomes too bad. Do not rub frostbitten areas; more pain and damage will be the result.

STEP 3 Protect that tissue from refreezing at all costs. Make sure to monitor the victim (or yourself) for signs of hypothermia (see item 130) and shock, as well.

136 PRODUCE A PROBE

Since the wind can build drifts over deep holes in the snow, hiding them from view, you should have a pole that can act as a probe in deep and uneven snowpack. The probe can also be used as a walking stick, a staff for self-defense, and even a pole for ice fishing—altogether, it's a lifesaver. Cut a sapling tree that is strong and straight, with a sturdy section that is about your height. One end can be sharpened, though it's not necessary. Use the probe by sticking it into the snow to test prospective places to step. If you feel a void or section of less resistance, don't step there! A probing tool like this can be vital when crossing glaciers and other terrain that commonly have holes, crevasses, water under the snow, and other hazardous features.

137 ASSESS THE ICE

To decide whether an ice-covered waterway is safe to traverse, you'll need to know the ice thickness. Using a cordless drill with a long paddle bit and a tape measure, drill a test hole and measure it. If the ice is less than 2 inches (5 cm) thick, stay off! The weight of a person can easily break through it. 4-inch (10-cm) ice (or thicker) is usually safe for walking, skating, and ice fishing on foot. 5-inch (12.5-cm) and thicker ice is probably safe for ATV or snowmobiling. 8- to 12-inch (20- to 30-cm) and thicker ice is probably safe for small cars or light pickups. Note that the words "probably " and "usually" were thrown around quite a bit. Any patch of ice can have thin spots, often due to warmer spring water or geothermal activity under the surface. And old ice, cloudy ice, and spring ice can be unpredictable and very dangerous, despite being thick. Go out only on clear, thick ice. Above all, remember this: If in doubt, don't try it out.

138

STUFF YOUR CLOTHES

In the event that your clothes do not offer enough insulation, use one of the oldest tricks in the book and stuff them. The goal is to create dead air space around your body so the elements cannot strip away your body heat so quickly. Use leaves, grass, moss, ferns, pine needles, bark fibers, and weed tops for insulation. It's a bit prickly, but do you want to be comfortable or do you want to be frozen? The stuffing can be live or dead material (dead is better) and wet or dry—but if you are already hypothermic, you'll need dry.

Ideally you'll have a loose-fitting outer layer so the stuffing isn't directly against your skin—but if you only have one layer, you'll have to make do. Tuck your pants into your socks, undo your pants, fill both legs with insulation on all sides, and then get your pants secured again. Tuck in your shirt and fill the front, back, and both sleeves with insulation. Pull on a hood or hat. You should now look like a scarecrow—this getup is admittedly itchy, prickly, crunchy, and ridiculous-looking, but it just might save your life.

139 FOLLOW DOS AND DON'TS

There's a small nervous feeling most people have when they venture out on a floating sheet of frozen water. I'm sure our ancestors felt it, and the cautious (or lucky) ones passed it down to us. As for the people who trod upon the ice without fear or hesitation—well, let's just say that they're outnumbered by a large margin, and for good reason. Listen to that little voice of caution and avoid ending up on thin ice—literally.

DO	DON'T
Wear a personal flotation device (PFD) under your winter clothes—unless you're driving on the ice as the excess bulk may keep you from escaping a sinking vehicle.	Never go out on the ice by yourself.
Carry ice rescue tools with you always. Keep them where they would be easy to reach if you end up in the water.	Never forget that spring ice is NEVER safe ice.
Have a very long length of rope that's easy to access for speedy rescues.	Never test the ice by walking out without a proper plan.

140 STAY ON TOP OF THIN ICE

Crossing a frozen lake or pond is one of the most dangerous outdoor activities. It's especially perilous toward the end of winter, when the ice pack is deteriorating and thickness alone is not an accurate gauge of safety. Here's how to walk on ice safely:

Stay away from inlet and outlet streams. Under-the-ice current can reduce ice strength by 20 percent or more.

Use your walking stick or ice chisel to test ice conditions.

Slushiness is a sign of a weakening pack; so is finding snow cover or water on top of ice. Depressions in the snow indicate a spring.

Tow your equipment sled on a long rope. You can push it toward a victim who has fallen through.

A nice long cord wrapped around an empty plastic jug makes a handy flotation device. Stand on sturdy ice and toss the jug to the victim.

Open water is a red flag, pointing to a marginal ice pack nearer the shore.

Beware of black, gray, or milky ice. It lacks the strength of clear blue or green ice.

Eroded shore ice is a sign of a thinning ice pack. Beware.

Ice sloping from a bank may trap air underneath, reducing its strength.

Pressure ridges are caused by fluctuating temperatures. Avoid them.

Thin cracks may let you see whether the ice is thick or not.

141

MAKE SAFETY SPIKES TO SAVE YOUR LIFE

Say "hard water" in northern regions, and folks know you're not complaining about rinsing soap out of your hair. In these cold climes, hard water is ice—as in ice fishing. And up here, you'd better know how to climb out when the water is not as hard as you thought. Here's a handy self-rescue device that has saved many a life.

HOW IT'S DONE Cut two 5-inch (12.7-cm) sections from a broomstick or 1-inch (2.5-cm) wooden dowel. On each of the pieces, drill a hole into one end that's slightly smaller than the diameter of whatever nails you have handy and another hole crosswise at the other end. Drive a nail into each end hole. Cut off the nailhead, leaving 1

inch of protruding nail. Sharpen with a file to a semisharp point. Thread a 6-foot (1.8-m) length (or equal to your arm span) of parachute cord through the crosswise holes and tie off with stopper knots. Thread one dowel through both coat sleeves. When you slip the coat on, keep the dowels just below your cuffs. If you go through the ice, grab the dowels and drive the nails into the ice to drag yourself out.

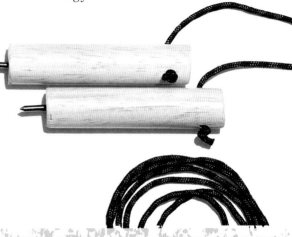

142

SURVIVE A FALL THROUGH ICE

FORGET HYPOTHERMIA The first thing to worry about when you've fallen into ice is getting yourself out. Assuming you have your safety spikes (see item 141), here's what to do.

STEP 1 Turn around in the water so you're facing the way you came. That's probably the strongest ice.

STEP 2 Jam the points of the spikes into the ice.

STEP 3 While kicking your feet vigorously, haul yourself out.

STEP 4 As soon as you're on the ice quickly roll (don't crawl) away from the edge of the hole. Get off the ice, and get warm immediately however you can.

143

BUILD A SURVIVAL SHELTER

In a winter wilderness emergency, shelter is going to be your top priority. If you find yourself wet or poorly dressed, hypothermia can begin to take hold within minutes, and, in harsh conditions, death can occur within a few hours. Thankfully, there are a number of survival shelter designs that can be built with few tools (or none at all) and made suitable for any landscape.

CREATE A LEAF HUT Winter isn't always about ice and snow; sometimes it's just bone-chillingly cold. In the event that there isn't any snow to fashion a shelter, build a nest out of available sticks, leaves, grasses, and other vegetation. You don't need tools—simply build a small bundle of natural materials in which you can just fit. Make it thick and fluffy to fight against the coldest weather.

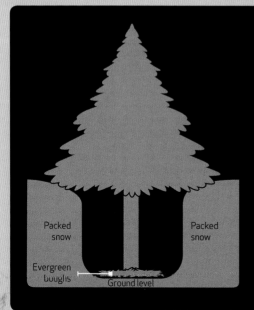

Packed snow

Packed snow

Evergreen boughs

Ground level

USE A TREE WELL In woodlands with deep snow, shelter can be as easy as a naturally occurring tree well. These are areas of lower snow density under the shelter of evergreen trees. When the snow collects on the tree boughs (rather than under the tree), it creates a natural pit that can be easily adapted into a shelter. Dig down to the bare ground, if possible, and use the snow to fill in gaps around the rim of the well. Since a fire in this shelter would melt the snow covering the boughs overhead, your best bet for warmth is packing the cavity with insulating materials. If you can manage to find a few rocks in the snow, use a fire to warm them and place them in your bedding as heaters.

DIG A SNOW CAVE When snow has drifted and frozen into a solid mass, you can excavate an excellent shelter using a shovel, large pot, or even your gloved hands. Add ventilation holes and a "cold well" to give the colder air a place to fall. Use a backpack or block of snow for a door, and—with any of these shelters—pile up a deep bed of evergreen boughs or other insulating material.

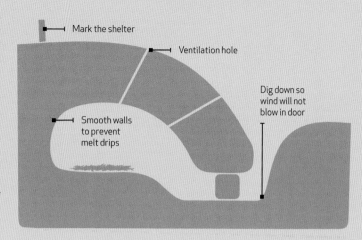

Mark the shelter

Ventilation hole

Dig down so wind will not blow in door

Smooth walls to prevent melt drips

BUILD A QUINZEE In wet, packable snow, a quinzee is a cozy group shelter. Pile up some gear (or snow) and cover it with a tarp; mound and pack more snow on top and insert sticks in the mound. Sticks should all be an equal length of 12–18 inches (30–45 cm). Let the pile harden a few hours, then dig a doorway, pull out the gear (or initial snow pile), and excavate as you would a cave. Stop digging when you start to hit the sticks—which will prevent thin spots in the dome. Add a door and you're all set.

BUILD A SNOW TRENCH Use a saw to cut slabs out of solid snow, creating a trench and ceiling blocks. You can dig out a trench in softer snow, too, and cover it with a roof of poles, tree boughs, and an insulating layer of snow. This trench is ideal for a one- or two-person shelter.

LAY BLOCKS FOR AN IGLOO The most impressive shelter is the igloo, an engineering masterpiece of carved blocks set in a spiraling dome. When properly built with the right quality of snow, the inside can reach temperatures above freezing from mere body heat. Start with a triangle-shaped block, then move to trapezoidal blocks, all with tapered edges. The final block is the keystone piece in the center. Amateurs can build an igloo if they're good with their hands (and with geometry), but the structures will never reach the quality of those made by one who regularly practices these crucial skills.

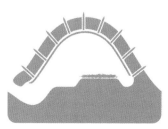

144 EAT A WINTER FEAST

Due to the short, chilly summer and long, deep winter, it's not possible to grow food crops in the Arctic. But the Inuit have always been hunters and anglers, relying heavily on high-calorie animal foods to survive.

In an ancestral diet, as much as 75% of the daily energy intake comes from fat (seems counterintuitive for a healthy diet, but you can't argue with the facts). Here's a traditional menu from a place that's too cold to farm.

FISH play a big role in ancient and modern diets.

ARCTIC BIRDS are a numerous species that provide meat, eggs, and feathers.

ARCTIC HARE AND FOX have both ended up in many an Arctic stew pot.

SEALS are hunted for meat and fur, and the liver has a higher level of vitamin C than many other animal foods.

POLAR BEARS are hunted for food and as predator control. Polar bear liver can be dangerously high in vitamin A.

WILD PLANTS harvested in summer and dried for winter include the Arctic's edible tubers, roots, berries, and seaweed for needed variety.

WALRUS are less desirable than seal (and more dangerous), but are still eaten today. Go easy on the liver, as its high vitamin A levels can be fatal.

WHALES such as beluga and bowhead are still hunted for food. One juvenile whale can feed a community for months.

CARIBOU AND MUSK OX are valuable for meat, fat, organs, and hide.

145

PUNCH A POLAR BEAR

In July 2010, 67-year-old Wes Werbowy had a very unusual encounter with a polar bear, and he prevented the animal's attack by punching the bear in the face—a last-ditch survival technique he learned from an Inuit elder.

Werbowy, a longtime wilderness consultant, was camping near Whale Cove, Nunavut, where he was training three Inuit hunters to be eco-tour guides. The four men had set up a camp, with separate sleeping and cooking tents to minimize the chances of a bear attack while they slept. Apparently, that wasn't effective, because just after 3 a.m. Werbowy awoke to the sound of a polar bear snuffling around outside his tent. The front of his tent collapsed as the bear pushed his head inside—the bear was less than a meter from Werbowy's face and standing on his gun. It's then that Werbowy recalled something that an Inuit elder once told him to do: punch a polar bear in the nose. Believing this might be his end, he held nothing back and slugged the massive white beast in its tender black nose. "I quite believed it was going to be the last thing I ever did, so I might as well do a good job," he said. The bear withdrew and disappeared. When the story went public, local elders praised Werbowy's bravery and wanted to shake the hand that punched a polar bear. The elders also believed that Werbowy performed a great service to the community. That bear would not be likely to approach humans again.

Obviously, a little prevention is a safer strategy than waiting to see if a solid sock in the nose will work. It's always best to travel in groups in polar bear country. Stay alert to your surroundings and set up a tripwire perimeter around your camp at night. Steer clear of female bears with cubs; they may attack in defense of their young. And keep food out of the equation by storing all food and garbage in bearproof containers outside your camp area. Finally, stay away from seals; these are the polar bear's primary food source.

146

PACK SOME BEAR SPRAY

Contrary to the name, bear spray isn't just for bears. It can be used on all kinds of two-legged and four-legged threats. Certainly a useful item for bear country, it's also a safety net for any other landscape in which you're not at the top of the food chain. Get the best bear spray that money can buy by ensuring that it's EPA-registered, sprays over 25 feet (8 m), and has an orange colorant. Color is a deterrent to intelligent creatures such as bruins, who are instinctively afraid of new things. They are not accustomed to an orange stinging cloud in their face, so they'll run off, then look back, trying to figure out what just happened. Meanwhile, you should be moving the other way. When used against a smaller predator, employ the same technique: Spray him in the face and get away while he's disoriented. A good policy with any threatening beast is to unload only half the canister. Save some spray for a backup shot.

147 NAVIGATE DESERT SANDS

Traveling the desert on foot is daunting. Not only are you dealing with dryness and temperature extremes, but also the landscape itself deceives. Watch out for these:

DECEPTIVE DISTANCES The clear air and lack of landmarks trick the eye, confusing estimates of distance. Be aware that faraway objects appear to be closer—it's the opposite of your car's side-view mirror.

TREACHEROUS TRAPS Although the way ahead may look level, the topography could be hiding incredibly dangerous ravines with sheer cliffs. And the desert sometimes conceals other hazards, like quicksand in dry streambeds. The same creeks may become raging torrents when a flash flood sweeps through the area, fed by a distant thunderstorm you didn't even know was happening.

LEGENDARY ILLUSIONS In the heat of the day, a mirage might appear, luring the unwary hiker to march toward imaginary water. Don't let that hiker be you. When mirages appear, that's the time to hunker down.

Stop walking, get hydrated, and rest in the shade, and that image of water will disappear, leaving your head clear enough so you can move on. To distinguish between a mirage and the real deal, all you have to do is look for surrounding vegetation, which will be thick and tall and green in the presence of water.

SEAFARERS' TIP Move through the desert the way you would move through the ocean. If you travel at night—when it is cooler—you can use stars as your fixed points. Rely only on solid landmarks such as mountain peaks (which remain visible in just a little moonlight) for navigation.

148 AVOID SCORPIONS

As with most of life's unpleasant circumstances, prevention is better than cure. To keep a scorpion from stinging you, be careful where you place your hands and where you sit or lie down when you're in scorpion territory. Be cautious when picking up anything that's been lying on the ground, including your sleeping bag and firewood. Before putting on clothing and footwear, shake them out to make sure a crusty buddy hasn't crawled inside. Scorpions love to hide in dark, cool places.

149 TREAT A SCORPION STING

If you didn't heed the advice in item 148 (or you were simply surprised), here's how to limit the damage from a sting.

STEP 1 If you have access to soap and water, wash the affected area.

STEP 2 Apply a cool compress to help reduce swelling and improve circulation.

STEP 3 If you are stung on an arm or a leg, elevate the limb to heart level if you can.

STEP 4 Keep your cool and try to relax as best you can. Thankfully, few victims of scorpion stings die, though you may experience unpleasant physical symptoms like rapid breathing, increased heart rate, and muscle weakness.

150 TREAT A SNAKE BITE

Snake bites happen all the time. And even a bite from a so-called harmless snake can cause infection or an allergic reaction. If you're bitten, the best course of action is to get emergency medical assistance as soon as you can. In the meantime, do the following:

STEP 1 Wash the bite with soap and water.

STEP 2 Immobilize the bitten area and, if possible, keep it lower than the heart.

STEP 3 Cover the area with a clean, cool compress or a moist dressing to minimize swelling and discomfort.

STEP 4 Monitor vital signs, such as temperature and pulse rate.

STEP 5 If you can't reach emergency medical care within 30 minutes—and if you are out in the wilderness, that is likely—place a suction device over the bite to help draw venom up out of the wound. Use your mouth to suck out the venom only as a last resort—and be sure to spit it out. Then wrap a bandage 2 to 4 inches (4 to 10 cm) above the bite to help slow the venom's movement. Don't totally cut off circulation—the bandage should be loose enough that you can slip a finger under it.

151 SPIT-ROAST A RABBIT

A caveman and cowboy movie cliché, spit roasting is one of the simplest cooking methods and ideal for small game like rabbit and squirrel. For the spit, choose wood like green oak or hickory that won't give a bad taste to the food. Ideally, the stick has a fork at one end that you can use for turning. Sharpen the other end to push through the meat. Shave the middle to flatten it along two opposite sides (this prevents the stick from rotating inside the food, so you're rotating the meat, not just the stick). Baste the meat with drippings caught in a pan (if you have one) or on some tree bark.

152 SKIN AND COOK A SNAKE

Mr. No Shoulders might give you the willies, but in a dire situation, a hot meal of snake meat might also give you enough energy to make it back to civilization. This should be a last resort. Some of these slithery creatures are protected.

STEP 1 Cut off the snake's head. Next, insert the knife tip into the anal vent and run the blade all the way up the belly.

STEP 2 Free a section of the skin. Grasp the snake in one hand, the freed skin section in the other, and pull the two apart; discard skin.

STEP 3 Remove all of the entrails, which lie along the base of the spine, and discard them.

STEP 4 Chop the meat into bite-size pieces. Cook by frying or boiling over a campfire.

153 MAXIMIZE A FIRE'S HEAT

The problem with campfires is that most of the heat escapes, so the fire warms only the side of your body that faces the flames. The ideal is to build a fire between two reflective surfaces and then station yourself in between them so you can absorb warmth. Set up a campfire 6 to 8 feet (1.8 to 2.4 m) from a natural reflector, such as a rock wall, then erect a stone or green log on the other side of the fire. Position yourself in the space between the fire and the wall and prepare to get toasty.

154 SEEK WATER IN A CANYON

Springs tend to surface at lower levels in canyons, so to find water, start near the canyon mouth and work your way upstream. Moving this way, up-canyon, is safer. It lessens the chance of descending a drop-off that you can't climb back up.

In addition to springs, look for "seeps"—moist spots in the canyon floor where water rises up from an underground source. Seeps often result in puddles substantial enough to drink from (although you should, of course, purify the water before doing so).

Beware of both pools and hot springs. Canyon-floor pools can be deceptively cold and deep and may be difficult to escape should you fall or jump in. The sulfurous fumes of hot springs can overcome you, and the water can be hot enough to literally boil you alive. Steer clear, no matter how tempting a nice warm wilderness bath might sound.

155

SCOUT FOR WATER IN THE DESERT

The desert is a place of such contrast that you can see any green vegetation at quite a distance. The leaves stand out from the rest of the neutral-colored and dry environment, like a drink of water just waiting to be gulped.

Tracking down rare lush patches that dot an otherwise arid landscape can help lead you to water. It might be below the surface, but it's there, and it's worth digging for. Scan the horizon; if you see a pattern of green, go to it. It might be grasses or even large trees, fed by an underground spring or puddles remaining from the last rains. Also keep an eye out for dampness near depressions of dry streambeds. If you find moisture, dig. Place the damp soil in a T-shirt, hold it overhead, and wring it to release water.

156 DEFEAT DEHYDRATION

We humans can go a while without food, but water is a whole different story. Without a constant supply of drinkable H2O, dehydration sets in quickly, along with low energy, poor judgment, and the eventual loss of the will to survive—not a good thing in my book.

DRINK ALL THE TIME Don't wait until you're thirsty to drink. Put yourself on a schedule and stick to it. And always have purified water on hand.

AVOID ASSUMPTIONS Little-known fact: Your risk of dehydration is just as high in the cold as it is in the heat.

Every breath you take releases moisture into the dry air, and when it's cold, you're probably less thirsty, so your instinct to drink water is hampered.

CHECK THE ELEVATION We all know that activity in the heat leads to dehydration if we don't drink enough water. But it's worse at high elevation: The air is arid and thin, so you're breathing hard and sweating more.

REPLACE FLUIDS If you do start experiencing signs of dehydration, drink clear fluids, such as water, clear broths, and electrolyte-containing beverages.

FIGHT DEHYDRATION IN THE DESERT

The desert is a land of dangerous extremes—it can kill you with its heat or its cold—but the biggest threat is the dryness. Dehydration can take you down in a matter of hours.

WATCH THE SIGNS The symptoms come slowly, and unless you're paying attention, you won't notice them. Your blood thickens and your body's blood volume is reduced. Your pulse speeds up and your heart works harder. You become exhausted. Your mind ceases to function well, and you begin to make bad decisions. Even without mistakes, death comes soon enough, unless you can find water and drink your fill.

KEEP COOL Try to pace your activities so you don't perspire too much. Seek the shade when the sun is hot. Travel only during the cool early morning and late evening hours, then rest overnight so you're not stumbling around in the darkness.

DRINK UP Store your water in your stomach, not your canteen. Contrary to popular belief, rationing water will not extend your life. Don't eat unless you have some water to drink. The digestion of food requires water in your system. Eating without water will dehydrate you faster. If you get desperate for water, filter and drink your urine as a last resort.

STAVE OFF THE COLD Dehydration can make hypothermia worse, and the desert can be bitterly cold at night. Find shelter before dark, get a fire started, and stay warm.

158 MAKE A SOLAR STILL

The solar still is a simple invention that collects water and distills it through a greenhouse effect. It's not perfect, nor does it collect massive quantities of water, but it does provide fresh water in arid climates and it can effectively desalinate saltwater.

In the original method developed in the 1970s, a square of clear or milky plastic is draped over a pit with a clean cup in the bottom. The plastic at the edge of the pit is sealed with a rim of dirt or stones to keep any of the steam from escaping. The plastic sheet is weighted down in the middle with a small rock, pushed down to shape the plastic into a cone shape. The sun will create a steamy environment under the plastic, and the steam will condense on the underside, running down into the cup below. Each site works for days, and you may get a up to a liter of water per still per day. Follow these tips to collect the most water.

TIP 1 Set up the still in a sunny area with the dampest dirt or sand available.

TIP 2 Make certain that the point of the cone of plastic is directly over the container inside the still.

TIP 3 Add vegetation inside to increase production.

TIP 4 Urine can be recycled by peeing down a hole dug next to the still so the liquid can soak through the ground and vaporize into the still.

TIP 5 A rubber, plastic, or vinyl drinking tube can be placed in the cup and lead outside the still. This way, water can be sipped as it collects without having to take the whole still apart to get the water out.

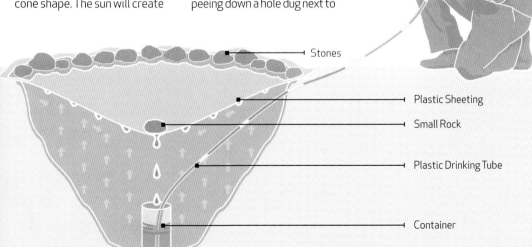

Stones

Plastic Sheeting

Small Rock

Plastic Drinking Tube

Container

159 SURVIVE HEAT ILLNESSES

There's heat, and then there's extreme heat—the kind that skyrockets your body temperature to 104°F (40°C), making you dizzy and hot to the touch and even rendering you unconscious. Here are some of the warning signs of heat exhaustion and heatstroke.

HEAT EXHAUSTION The milder of the two heat-caused ailments, heat exhaustion occurs when the body's temperature gets too high. People affected with heat exhaustion experience physical symptoms such as dizziness, nausea, fatigue, heavy sweating, and clammy skin. The treatment is simple: Have the victim lie down in the shade, elevate his or her feet, and supply plenty of fluids.

HEATSTROKE If someone's body temperature reaches 104°F (40°C), that person needs immediate treatment for heatstroke, which can be deadly. Besides an alarming thermometer reading, the easiest signs to identify are hot, dry skin; headache; dizziness; and unconsciousness. To treat, elevate the victim's head and wrap him or her in a wet sheet. If you can get to one, go to a hospital. Heatstroke can damage the kidneys, brain, and heart if it goes on for too long.

160

SCALE A CANYON

Stuck in a canyon? Take a tip from Santa and shimmy up a chimney. A narrow slot is sometimes the only escape route. The trick to climbing it is to use opposing forces.

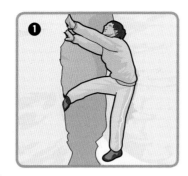

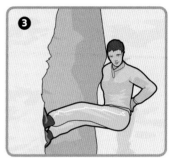

STEP 1 Put your back to one wall of the chimney and one foot about knee-high against the wall in front of you.

STEP 2 Place your other foot on the wall behind you, bending your knee. Put your hands behind your back.

STEP 3 Push up with your legs and arms, straightening your bent leg and "stepping" up the chimney wall. Then repeat, stepping up with your other leg until you're at the top.

161 DESCEND A CLIFF

If you have to rappel down a cliff with a single rope, you won't get a second chance to do it right. Take notes.

CHOOSE AN ANCHOR POINT This can be a sturdy tree or rock outcrop near the edge of the precipice. Make sure the anchor point won't pinch the rope as you pull it down from below. Pass the rope around the anchor so that the two ends are even and meet the landing point with a few feet of extra rope.

WRAP YOUR BODY With your back to the cliff, straddle the double strand of rope. Pass it around your right hip and then across your chest and over your left shoulder. Grasp the ropes at your lower back with your right hand, and bring them around to your right hip. With your left hand, grasp the ropes in front at chest height.

DESCEND Keeping close to perpendicular to the cliff, walk down the precipice. Relax your grips periodically to slide down the rope. To arrest a swift descent, grip tightly with your right hand while pulling the rope to the front of your waist. At the bottom, retrieve the rope by pulling one end.

INDEX

INDEX

INDEX

ABOUT THE MAGAZINE

Since its founding in 1898, *Outdoor Life* magazine has provided survival tips, wilderness skills, gear reports, and other essential information for hands-on outdoor enthusiasts. Each issue delivers the best advice in sportsmanship as well as thrilling true-life tales; detailed gear reviews, insider hunting, shooting, and fishing hints, and much more to nearly 1 million readers. Its survival-themed website also covers disaster preparedness and the skills needed to thrive anywhere—from the backcountry to urban jungles.

CREDITS

Waterbury Publications, Inc., Des Moines, IA

Creative Director Ken Carlson
Editorial Director Lisa Kingsley
Associate Design Director Doug Samuelson
Associate Editor Tricia Bergman
Production Designer Mindy Samuelson
Copy Editor Peg Smith
Proofreader Gretchen Kauffman
Indexer Kevin Broccoli

Photography courtesy of *Shutterstock Images* except where otherwise noted: *Alamy:* 157 *Peter Barrot/Digital Studio:* 22 *Bill Buckley:* Table of contents (Elk bull) *Eddie Berman:* 94 *Brad Fenson:* 76 *Cliff Gardiner and John Keller:* 3 (a, c, d, f, k, l), 18, 24 (Cedar bark, tinder fungus), 32 *Getty Images:* 148 *iStockphoto:* 37, 104 (Poison oak), 152 *Alexander Ivanov:* Index (Recurve Knife), 3 (g, j), 9, 24 (duct tape, egg carton and sawdust, cottonballs and petroleum jelly, flare, tube, dryer lint, Spanish moss, birch bark, sagebrush bark, punk wood, cattail fluff) *Donald M. Jones:* 8 *Pippia Morris:* 3 (h) *Ted Morrison:* 124 *T. Edward Nickens:* 3 (i), closing pages (birds over lake) *Pelican Products Inc.:* 26 *Travis Rathbone:* 141 *Dan Saelinger:* 12, 100 *Dusan Smetana:* Table of contents (person starting fire), table of contents (man in forest), 46, Lost in the Woods closing image (man in forest)

Illustrations courtesy of *Conor Buckley:* 1, 2, 21, 30, 48, 61, 68, 77, 85, 90, 93, 98, 106, 122, 128, 131, 135, 137, 140, 143, 144, 145, 151 *Liberum Donum:* 127, 160 *Hayden Foell:* 54, 56, 82, 110, 112 *Joshua Kemble:* 50 *Raymond Larrett:* 38, 58, 95, 111 *Daniel Marsiglio:* 10, 41, 43, 84, 115, 126, 142 *Robert L. Prince:* 19 *Jameson Simpson:* 34, 39, 71 *Jaime Spinello:* 27, 29, 72, 102, 116 *Mike Sudal:* 121 *Bryon Thompson:* 45, 65, 89, 107, 158 *Lauren Towner:* 20, 25, 42, 124 *Paul Williams:* 15, 33 *Waterbury Publications, Inc.:* Chapter intro icons

weldon**owen**

President & Publisher Roger Shaw
SVP, Sales & Marketing Amy Kaneko
Finance & Operations Philip Paulick
Associate Publisher Mariah Bear
Editor Ian Cannon
Editorial Assistant Molly O'Neill Stewart
Creative Director Kelly Booth
Art Director Allister Fein
Senior Production Designer Rachel Lopez Metzger
Illustration Coordinator Conor Buckley
Production Director Chris Hemesath
Associate Production Director Michelle Duggan
Imaging Manager Don Hill

Weldon Owen would like to thank Waterbury Publications, Des Moines, IA, for layout and production.

© 2016 Weldon Owen Inc.
1045 Sansome Street, suite 100
San Francisco, CA 94111
www.weldonowen.com

BONNIER

ISBN 13: 978-1-68188-151-5
ISBN 10: 1-68188-151-9
10 9 8 7 6 5 4 3 2 1
2015 2016 2017 2018
Printed in China by RR Donnelley

OUTDOORLIFE

Vice President, Publishing Director Gregory D. Gatto
Editorial Director Anthony Licata
Editor-in-Chief Andrew McKean
Executive Editor John Taranto
Managing Editor Jean McKenna
Senior Deputy Editor John B. Snow
Deputy Editor Gerry Bethge
Assistant Managing Editor Margaret M. Nussey
Assistant Editor Natalie Krebs

Senior Administrative Assistant Maribel Martin
Design Director Sean Johnston
Art Director Brian Struble
Associate Art Directors Russ Smith, James A. Walsh
Photography Director John Toolan
Photo Editor Justin Appenzeller
Production Manager Judith Weber
Digital Director Nate Matthews
Online Content Editor Alex Robinson